D0717690

The Liffey

~ Portrait of a River ~

Text by Dick Warner

Paintings by Rosemary Burns

Cottage
Publications

First published by Cottage Publications,
an imprint of Laurel Cottage Ltd.
Donaghadee, N. Ireland 2007.
Copyrights Reserved.
© Illustrations by Rosemary Burns 2007.
© Text by Dick Warner 2007.
All rights reserved.
No part of this book may be reproduced or stored on any media
without the express written permission of the publishers.
Design & Origination in Northern Ireland.
Printed & bound in China.
ISBN 978 1 9009 3562 3

Rosemary Burns has been living in Kildare for the past 30 years. The many contrasts of the Irish landscape have always inspired Rosemary's water-colour painting and so was very excited at the prospect of portraying the river Liffey and all its aspects for this book.

A well known watercolour artist Rosemary studied Art & Design as a mature student at the national College of Art and Design and graduated in 1994 with a B.Des.Hons.

When not at her easel Rosemary can be found teaching keen enthusiasts how to paint at one of her many watercolour holidays held annually at some beautiful locations including Connemara, Spain Croatia and Vienna.

Rosemary's work is included in many private and corporate collections in Ireland and abroad.

Examples can be viewed at www.arc-designs.ie

Dick Warner is a writer, broadcaster and environmentalist. He writes on subjects as diverse as inland waterways, angling in Ireland and the identification of trees and is a regular contributor to several newspapers and magazines on topics to do with the environment and wildlife. He has made a number of television documentary series that have been shown all over the world. These include *Waterways*, on Ireland's inland waterways; *Spirit of Trees* about trees; *Voyage*, a circumnavigation of Ireland in a sailing yacht and *Ironing The Land* on the history of Irish railways. He also writes television scripts for other presenters and is a regular radio broadcaster.

Dick worked as a producer for RTE for over twenty years but is now self-employed and lives, with his wife and two children, on a small-holding in Co Kildare. He grows organic vegetables and keeps poultry and pigs and is partially self-sufficient. The whole Warner family has a great love of boats and spend a lot of time on their inland waterways cruiser.

Contents and Illustrations

Introduction   7

Source to Poulaphouca   9

    Curious Deer at the Sally Gap   11
    Young river dances to the morning sunrise   13
    Meandering river through Coronation Plantation   15
    Taking a dip at Ballysmuttan   19
    Gushing waters at Clochlea   23
    Greylags at Dawn over Blessington Lake   27

Poulaphouca to Chapelizod   37

    Challenging times, Liffey Descent   39
    Casting near the Old Mill at Ballymore Eustace   41
    Ancient Monastic settlement, Old Kilcullen   45
    Early morning gallop on the Curragh   47
    Bridge at Athgarvan   49
    Droichead Nua at Newbridge   51
    Early morning stroll, 'Strand' at Newbridge   53
    Restored Mill Wheel at Morristown Lattin   57
    Tranquility at the Old Weir Victoria Bridge   59
    A passage in time -Leinster Aquaduct - Sallins   61

    Mirrors of time near the K-Club, Straffan   65
    Lovers' retreat, Celbridge Abbey   67
    Evening paddlers, Leixlip canoe club   69
    Autumnal hues, Leixlip Dam   71
    Winter sunshine, Lucan Village   73
    Awaiting owners near pub in Chapelizod   77
    Before the 'Off' –Trinity Rowing Club   78

Through Dublin to the Sea   81

    Heuston Station & Dr Steevens Hostpital   87
    Glass o' Porter! Guinness Brewery   89
    Striking a deal, Smithfield Horse Fair   93
    The Liffey Boardwalk   97
    Capel Street towards Essex Quay and Dublin Castle   99
    Equinox sunset, Ha'penny Bridge   101
    Liberty Hall and O'Connell Bridge   103
    Midnight reflections, Customs House   105
    Heritage boats at the redeveloped campshires   107
    Enjoying the amenities of the South Wall   109
    Evening Solitude At Clontarf   110

It takes a lot of work to write a book. When I finish one I normally say "never again". But this one just had to be written. I have known and loved the Liffey for most of my life and for the past twenty-five years I have lived close to its middle reaches in County Kildare. I have canoed on it, fished in it, watched its wildlife and explored it from source to mouth.

I've always had a passion for things watery and I've no idea where it came from. I'm actually a poor swimmer with a mild fear of drowning. But I just can't keep away from lakes and the sea shore, from canals, streams and rivers. Rivers are really the best of all because they're so dynamic and because they change so much as they grow from source to mouth. And the Liffey is very special among rivers.

Because it's the river of the capital city it's unusually rich in history and culture. It's James Joyce's river and the heroine of Finnegan's Wake. It's also Viking Dublin's river and the boundary, so important to Dubliners, between north-side and south-side. In addition it rises on a treeless mountainside in County Wicklow and flows through the rich farmland of County Kildare. This makes for a variety of landscapes and habitats along the banks and a particularly rich assortment of flora and fauna.

None of this makes the work any easier. Having too much material is actually worse than having too little. A comprehensive book about the Liffey would run to many volumes. It would also require expert knowledge of history and geography, botany and zoology, architecture and literature, geology, archaeology and many other 'ologies' – this I don't have, and I'm not sure that there's anyone who does. I've had to approach things as an amateur and make personal choices – putting in information that interests, amuses or intrigues me and discarding the rest. This may be irritating to some people whose interests are different to mine but if so there is one consolation – the pictures.

I haven't known Rosemary for quite as long as I've known the Liffey but she lives not far away, in Newbridge, and I've been an admirer of her watercolours for many years. I think she has a great talent for interpreting the subtleties of our local landscapes. That's why I found the invitation to collaborate with her on portraits of the river irresistible.

I hope that what we have done will inspire people to go out themselves and discover more treasures along the course of this truly amazing waterway. The pleasure it has given me is there for everyone.

Bogland Beginnings
- River Liffey Source

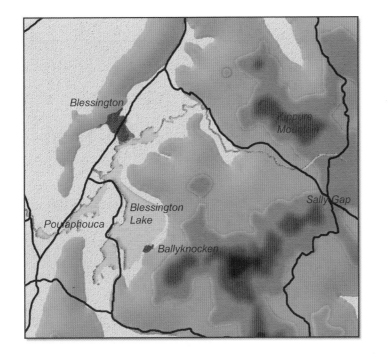

The source of a river is seldom spectacular. The Liffey is no exception. The actual source is a large, dark puddle on a gently sloping saddle of moorland between Kippure mountain and Tonduff mountain. It's in Wicklow but close to the boundary with County Dublin.

The source is marked on Ordnance Survey maps. If you want to find it and you're coming from the Dublin direction take the Military Road past Glencree and Lough Bray. About five hundred metres after the gateway that leads to the RTE transmission mast on Kippure you'll cross a small and inconspicuous bridge with low granite parapets. This is the rather grandly named 'Liffey Head Bridge'. Park at the closest safe point to the bridge and put on your wellies. Then walk eastwards, following the little streamlet, for about six hundred metres.

The source itself may be a bit of an anticlimax but the surroundings are magnificent. The expanse of moorland is as empty a wilderness as you'll find anywhere in Ireland and in a straight line it's little more than twenty kilometres from the centre of the capital city.

This is upland blanket bog, a rare landscape type in international terms and one that, in a pure and undamaged form, is diminishing in Ireland. It's called a blanket bog because the peat, anything up to two metres deep around here, cloaks the underlying rock like a blanket, following the contours of the land. A raised bog, in comparison, builds up in a dome that does not reflect the contours beneath.

The courses of the infant Liffey and its first tiny tributaries appear as green lines scribbled across the brown bog. The green comes from several species of grass, rush and moss. In winter floods the stream erodes the peat, exposing the bedrock and scraps of mineral soil beneath. The green plants can exploit this niche.

On the surrounding peat the two main plant species are ling heather and cotton grass, or bog cotton. The ling

colonises the drier ground and the bog cotton the damp places. At most times of the year they appear brownish in the distance. In fact the bog cotton produces its bright white tufts in early summer and its stems turn dark red in autumn and the ling produces a mass of purple flowers in late summer. There are other lovely

Bog Cotton

flowering plants up here as well, including some patches of bog asphodel with striking flowers, yellow tinged with red, appearing in July.

A close look at the stream bed will reveal information about the geology under the peat. Where gravel collects it will be granite gravel and, if the sun is shining, it will glitter. The sparkle comes from scraps of mica and white quartz that have eroded out of the rock.

If you're lucky while you're up here you may hear, or even see, one of Ireland's endangered birds. The Irish red grouse has been declining steadily for the past century and current estimates put its numbers at between five hundred and two thousand pairs left in the whole country. This part of the north Wicklow uplands is one of its last strongholds.

Red grouse in Ireland were originally accorded the status of a separate sub-species or race, different to red grouse in other countries. There are a handful of other bird species that hold this honour, including the jay, dipper and coal tit, all of which are found at various locations along the Liffey. However grouse are, or were, important as game birds and, as they declined in Ireland, various sporting interests tried to augment the population with birds imported from Britain. Because of this it's doubtful whether the

Curious Deer at
The Sally Gap

subtle characteristics that made Irish grouse different to British ones still exist in our small remaining population.

The peat in the blanket bog acts like a giant sponge, releasing its water to the embryonic river and allowing it to grow rapidly. It soon turns into a true mountain stream, bouncing between boulders and leaping over rapids. And on the flanks of the hills beside it the first signs of human activity become apparent – the pure wilderness character is soon lost.

This upland peat has been harvested for fuel since prehistoric times. The activity peaked in the 1940s when wartime shortages forced us into self-sufficiency for fuel. Swarms of Dubliners tackled the gruelling uphill cycle ride from the city with sleans strapped to their crossbars and sandwiches and tea in their haversacks, intent on saving turf and saving the nation. Turf lorries were allowed a special petrol ration so the precious harvest was brought back to the city mechanically.

It was tough work but it seems to have struck some sort of atavistic chord in the people who did it. It was a way for city people to spend a few weeks in the summer re-connecting with their rural roots. Because even after the economic necessity receded the tradition of Dubliners, often middle-class Dubliners, coming up into these mountains

to save turf has continued. I did it myself once. The rights of turbary used to belong to the Powerscourt Estate and up until recently tractor powered 'sausage machines' extracted the turf, though it was still 'footed' by hand – turned and stacked to dry it out. But Powersourt has now sold the land to the State and turf cutting is no longer allowed for conservation reasons. The turf banks, old and new, can be seen as cicatrices on the sloping banks of the upper Liffey, wounds inflicted by Dubliners on the catchment of a river that, a hundred and twenty-five kilometres later, will grace their city.

And soon the Liffey crosses under the road that leads from the Sally Gap down towards Ballysmuttan and skirts the Coronation Plantation. If you arrive as a new explorer to the upper Liffey and expect the Coronation Plantation to look like a modern forestry plantation you're in for a surprise. What you'll see instead is a bare hillside dotted with irregular groves of Scots pine.

It started life as one of the earliest forestry plantations in the country, but it never succeeded and it was never finished. The starting date was 1831; the coronation it celebrated was that of King William IV of England.

In these pre-famine times our population was far larger than it is today and the vast bulk of the people were ten-

Near source - Young river dances to the morning sunrise

ants on huge estates. At one time nearly a quarter of our land area was owned by just ten men. Many of these landlords embarked on ambitious schemes to improve their estates and in many cases the motivation was to better the lot of the tenants as well as to increase their own income. The Coronation Plantation was just such a scheme.

In the 1830s American conifer species like Sitka spruce, Douglas fir and Lodgepole pine had not yet become available for large scale forestry plantation in Ireland. But Scots pine grew wild, as it still does today, in the Caledonian Pine Forest in the highlands of Scotland. No doubt these early foresters saw some similarities between the landscape of Wicklow and the Scottish highlands so it seemed a logical species to choose.

But the Scots pines in the Coronation Plantation are steadily dwindling in numbers. There is no natural regeneration. This is partly due to the fact that any young trees are browsed down by sheep, deer and hares. But it's also because natural regeneration in the highlands of Scotland depends on cones being blown across hard-packed snow and ice by high winds in winter. Scottish pine groves always spread down wind. The milder climate and lower altitude in Wicklow is less likely to provide these conditions.

Anyway, it's not very suitable as a plantation tree. In the wild it doesn't grow in dense canopy forests. It exploits niches that don't suit other species and grows in open groves with an under-storey of blueberry and heather. It's an unsociable tree and the groves are sparsely dotted over the open moorland.

The maximum natural life-span of a Scots pine is about three hundred and fifty years. This means that the trees planted in the 1830s are only middle-aged. But some have been felled and there is also natural wastage from wind-blow, fire and lightning strikes so, without regeneration, it looks as though the plantation is doomed.

The river, however, is growing in strength. The gradient has eased and the river bed has spread out. It's punctuated by boulders and some long beds of gravel – at least it is in dry conditions. After heavy rain it can go into a great spate, often rising by two or even three metres. This flattens the bracken and rushes along the banks and it can take them several weeks to struggle upright again. It also festoons the bank-side bushes of furze and sally with tresses of dead vegetation.

Back from the river the landscape is turning from moorland to farmland. It's not great farmland but it seems to have been popular for a very long time because there is

Meandering river
through Coronation
Plantation

evidence of the existence of Neolithic farmers in the vicinity over five thousand years ago.

The sites chosen by the first Stone Age farmers often seem rather illogical. The area of the Ceide Fields in northwest Mayo doesn't appear a sensible or profitable place to set up an agricultural enterprise and the same could be said for this area of the upper Liffey valley.

Admittedly the climate was a little different then and the landscape was very different. Farming actually started in Ireland before the main phase of bog growth, which is why the fields of Ceide are covered in peat.

But the main difference was that most of Ireland was a dense forest and this forest was both an enemy and a friend of the first farmers. It was an enemy because it harboured wild animals – wild pigs could eat all your crop in one night, wolves could kill your livestock and bears were capable of killing members of your family. The forest also had a dense canopy and the shade beneath was too dark to grow crops in.

Though foreboding, the forest had a deep, fertile soil made from centuries of leaf mould. Stone Age tools were not efficient enough to grub up the matted roots in grassland so the farmers were forced into the forest, or, at least, the forest fringe. Here they ring-barked larger trees and, when the leaves fell off, or failed to appear the following spring, they cultivated the loose soil in the patch of dappled sunlight they had created.

But they never ventured too deeply into the great forest. They lived on the margins. And this part of the upper Liffey valley was one of those margins. And they left some signs behind them.

To bury their dead they climbed Seefin mountain to the north east, well away from the dangers of the forest and their precarious settlement on its fringe. On the mountain they built a great burial mound with five chambers, a corbelled roof and a façade of glistening white quartz. And they carved mysterious lozenge shapes and other geometrical patterns on to blocks of stone.

The Seefin monument is contemporary with the famous ones at Newgrange, Knowth and Dowth in the Boyne Valley, though not as large and not as well preserved. There are other similar tombs overlooking the upper Liffey valley, on the mountains of Seefingan, Sorrell and Lugnagun.

Today agriculture is declining and the marginal lands are being abandoned or reverting to rough grazing for sheep. A tradition with nearly six thousand years of history looks

Inquisitive Deer Family

to be coming to an end. And the forest, in the form of dense plantations of American conifers, may be having the last laugh.

All the large wild animals that the Neolithic farmers contended with eventually became extinct in the Liffey valley. The last one to go was the red deer. This probably happened in the first half of the nineteenth century, though I can't find any precise references.

There was great pressure on wild animals in the hungry years before and during the Great Famine. Native red deer survived in Donegal until the 1860s and appear to have survived in west Mayo until the 1930s. In the Killarney region of Co. Kerry they never became extinct. Some experts have suggested that the Killarney herd may be descended from animals introduced into the country by the very same Neolithic farmers who built the passage tombs but modern genetic research indicates that they are more likely to be true native animals that were here before the arrival of the first humans.

Anyway in Co. Wicklow, close to the source of the Liffey, red deer were reintroduced soon after their extinction by Lord Powerscourt. I've seen a full-length portrait of him in his House of Lords regalia – modern day rap artists are very wrong if they think they invented bling. He had huge estates in Wicklow and an interest in animals so he imported British red deer at some time in the 1850s. Britain and Ireland were one country at the time, at least in the mind of Lord Powerscourt, so he had no conception that he was importing stock of foreign origin. Unfortunately shortly afterwards, in 1860, he added a second species to the collection in his deer park – the sika deer which is a distant and diminutive relation of the red deer originating in the Japanese Archipelago.

At the time nobody knew that the two species could interbreed and that the resulting hybrids would be fertile. But they can and they did and they also escaped. The result is that there are very large numbers of deer in Wicklow and the fringes of the surrounding counties today but probably no pure red deer, they're all either sikas or hybrids. Although there are no good census figures for deer numbers in Ireland the Wicklow herd is probably around fifteen thousand animals. Large numbers (between one and two thousand) are shot each year, legally and illegally, but the population is still increasing.

Many of the bridges across the Liffey are very beautiful structures but the one built across the old ford at Ballysmuttan in 1848 doesn't really fall into that category. The vertical piers are rather attractive because they're made of local granite, finely cut and fitted. But the span is a flat roadway of concrete and steel and the parapets are a rusting and dented lattice work of cast iron.

1848 is the height of the railway building age in Ireland and this bridge owes more to the utilitarian aesthetics of a rail bridge than it does to the architectural skills of the stone mason. Despite this Ballysmuttan is a popular place, particularly with Dublin families on fine summer Sunday afternoons.

There is parking space and the river in summer is too shallow to pose any danger to children playing in it. It can be paddled across, dams can be constructed on the narrow channels and stones can be skipped on the pools. There are also banks of coarse sand that provide a mountain substitute for beaches.

Many people who use this amenity probably don't realize that the Liffey at Ballysmuttan was once the site of an unusual and significant piece of Irish scientific research.

In the 1920s Dr. Rowland Southern was Assistant Director of Fisheries in Dublin and a world authority on trout. He was puzzled by the difficult but important question of why trout in some waters grow more quickly and end up larger than they do in others. The question was to become even more important later in the century with the extensive development of fish farming. He came up with the theory that the amount of calcium dissolved in the water and its resulting acidity or alkalinity were, either directly or indirectly, the key factors.

He had observed that trout from hard, alkaline water in limestone areas grew faster and larger than trout from soft, acid water in granite or sandstone areas. But he needed to do field work to test his theories and learn more about why the relative acidity of the water affected the growth of the fish. To do this he required samples of fish from two sites, one with acid water and one with alkaline, both of them within reasonable distance of his Dublin laboratory.

He chose Ballysmuttan as his acid water site and the Liffey at Straffan in Co. Kildare for his alkaline water samples. Unfortunately in 1935 the River Liffey Survey, as it was

*Taking a dip at
Ballysmuttan*

called, was just beginning to yield exciting results when Rowland Southern died prematurely at the age of fifty three. Dr. W. Frost, his young research assistant, was left to carry on the work.

This was unusual in the scientific context of the time because Dr. Frost was a young woman – the 'W' stood for Winifred. She later wrote:

> *I, a very junior colleague of Southern's, helped him in field and laboratory with his River Liffey Survey. The trout we needed for the work had to be caught by angling so Southern taught me how to fish with an artificial fly. This art has given me untold pleasure since and from its practice I have learned much about the trout in river and lake.*

She certainly did learn a lot because, very much later in her distinguished career, she collaborated with another outstanding woman biologist, Dr. Margaret Brown, to produce a monograph with the title *'The Natural History of the Brown Trout in the British Isles'*. It's a fairly dense scientific treatise, full of graphs and mathematical formulae, but in 1967 the Collins New Naturalist series published a popular version of it called *'The Trout'*. This became the standard work, and it still is. It's regularly consulted and

quoted from today by a wide range of people with an interest in fish.

Winifred Frost and Margaret Brown lived and worked in an era when there was still quite a lot of prejudice against women in the scientific community. This is probably why they always published material with only their initials in the authors' credit, concealing their first names. Most of the people who read their work probably never knew that it was done by two women.

I've never found a picture of either of them but I sometimes try and imagine what they looked like as they waded up the shallow river at Ballysmuttan with their split cane fly rods and their wicker creels. Did they change out of their long skirts into slacks to put their waders on, and did this ever scandalise some local sheep farmer?

Below Ballysmuttan the Liffey water still flows ale-coloured, stained by the peat. Its acidity, so important to Winifred Frost, owes as much to the humic acid trickling out of the bog, as it does to the acid rocks of the Wicklow uplands. Another more recent contributing factor is modern forestry. Conifer trees shed their needles in a steady, year round stream. As these needles decay they also produce humic acid which leaches into the water and makes it even more acid. Even the rain falling in the hills has become acidic. Sulphates and nitrates emitted from industrial plants and power stations in the west of Ireland form dilute nitric and sulphuric acid in the atmosphere and fall on Wicklow as acid rain.

But there is life in the river. The larger rocks are bare on top but, below the water line, they are coated with algae of a dark olive colour that supports a healthy population of invertebrates to feed the trout. The smaller stones are free of this growth. They are tumbled about so much in the frequent floods that they can't support life.

On land some of the stones have been built into field boundaries, others piled up into cairns that are monuments to past generations of hard-labouring, land hungry farmers trying to improve their holdings. Yet others litter the landscape just where the ice dropped them over ten thousand years ago. Unlike the river stones, the land ones are coloured by growths of lichen.

Lichens are an extraordinary life form. Each colony is a symbiosis between a fungus and either an alga or a bacterium. This relationship stretches back to the very dawn of life on earth. They are, on one level, very tough. Lichens make their living from chemicals slowly dissolved from the rock on which they grow and nutrients in the rain that falls on them. They don't demand much from their

environment and some species can probably live for thousands of years. But on another level they're very fragile. In particular they're vulnerable to even small amounts of air pollution.

Scientists from University College Dublin did a fascinating study after smokeless fuels became mandatory in the greater Dublin area. They mapped how the lichens slowly re-colonised the city as the air quality improved. You can be sure that if you have lichens growing near your home that the air is good to breathe.

As the Liffey continues down stream it enters something resembling an open gorge. The banks close in and so do the forestry plantations. Then, at Clochlea (also spelt 'Clochleagh') it's joined by its first major tributary, the Shankill River.

The Shankill is a delightful stream, particularly in the area around the bridge and church. It flows in a series of rapids and waterfalls through a thickly wooded glen. The wood is composed mostly of beech with some oak, Spanish chestnut and holly. It's the first decent wood of large deciduous trees in the Liffey valley. The Church of Ireland church is an attractive nineteenth century building on the site of an earlier one. It has a sexton's house beside it and a rectory across the road.

If you're a bird watcher and you were lucky enough to spot a grouse up near the source of the Liffey, this is quite a good area to add any one of the other three Irish endemic sub-species to your list. Coal tits and jays are found in the wood and dippers in the stream.

The boisterous Shankill eventually leaves the wood to join the more placid Liffey, which is meandering between gravel banks in the valley below. At the junction something interesting occurs, and something that shows that Rowland Southern knew his river well when he picked Ballysmuttan as one of the two sites for his River Liffey Survey. For the first time some of the boulders, stones and gravel in the river are composed of limestone.

This does not mean that the bedrock is changing, though we are coming close to the edge of the Wicklow granite. The nearest naturally occurring limestone is at Saggart, which is about ten kilometres to the north. These pieces of limestone are glacial erratics, lumps of rock that became embedded in a slow-moving glacier during the last Ice Age and were carried along and dumped here when the ice finally melted.

But limestone dissolves relatively rapidly in water and as these erratics gave up their calcium they started to change the river. The brown peat stain begins to leave the water and it is less strongly acidic. This affects the plants and animals that can live in it. New species demanding more nutrients can establish themselves and the trout are starting to grow a little faster and get a little bigger.

The river takes a sharp turn to the west around the foot of the Hill of Ballyfoyle. The landscape is now hilly rather than mountainous and the character of the river is changing too. It meanders through a flood plain of sweet grass. The farms are larger and more prosperous, and so are the farm houses.

Just south of Kilbride what appears to be a large tributary joins the Liffey from the north. But it's really a back-water not a tributary. The Ordnance Survey map of 1838 shows that this was then the main course of the river, which took a large meander. At some time between now and then, and I can't find out when it happened, the river burst its banks during a massive flood and took a short cut across the loop of the meander, creating its modern and shorter bed. It's quite interesting to try and work out the course of the old river bed.

A little further downstream the Liffey is joined by a true tributary, and an important one. The Brittas river is only about five kilometres long but its importance lies in the fact that its entire course is over limestone gravel. It's clear,

Gushing waters at
Clochlea

lime-rich water contributes further to lowering the Liffey's acidity and increasing the diversity of the animals and plants that can live in it. There is a cul-de-sac road leading down towards the junction of the two rivers which ends rather abruptly in the yard of a private house.

The Brittas river has a population of an interesting animal that is of international conservation importance. The white-clawed crayfish, our largest freshwater crustacean, is a small brownish-olive lobster – adults have a body length of about four centimetres. Biologists are divided on the question of whether it is a true native Irish species or whether it was introduced at an early date, possibly as a food item by medieval monks.

Over most of its European range this crayfish is extinct or seriously endangered. The reason is that they are valued as food in most countries, though they were not commonly eaten in Ireland. The white-clawed crayfish is slow-growing which makes it unsuitable for rearing in fish farms so crayfish growers imported faster growing species from abroad, particularly from North America. Unfortunately these imported crayfish carried a virus that the white-clawed crayfish had no resistance to and the virus escaped into the wild and wiped out the native species.

Shelled freshwater crayfish tails are sometimes available in Irish supermarkets but they are all imported because there are no crayfish farms in this country. This also means that we are the only country in which the white-clawed crayfish did not catch the virus, or at least we think we are.

Irish wild crayfish populations are declining. This could be because the virus has somehow sneaked into this country but there are probably other factors at work. The little lobsters are vulnerable to any decline in water quality and have recently acquired some new enemies.

Feral American mink have spread rapidly over the whole country in the past forty or fifty years and they love to eat crayfish, which they find relatively easy to catch. Crayfish are also a prized delicacy in the Baltic States and, although they are completely protected by law, recently there has been an increase in illegal fishing for them.

The river flows on, skirting the village of Kilbride, and reaches Ballyward Bridge. It was a very nice bridge when I was young. There was a graceful symmetry to the masonry, with a large round-headed arch flanked by two smaller ones. But in September 1986 Hurricane Charlie made an unexpected visit to Ireland and the central arch was swept away in the resulting flood. Wicklow County Council put in a temporary flat span to restore road access but the bridge was not replaced until 1993.

And now the river becomes broader and shallower as it approaches Blessington Lakes. The banks are steep and made up of glacial gravel containing practically every major rock type in Ireland.

The name Blessington Lakes is traditional but not totally logical because it's actually a single lake with three massive lobes that join in the middle. It looks on the map like a tattered and irregular clover leaf. It was created in 1940 when the dam at Poulaphouca was completed. This was a joint venture between Dublin Corporation (now Dublin City Council) and the ESB. It was designed to provide a new water supply for Dublin and north Kildare and to generate hydro-electricity. At the time it was the largest artificial reservoir in Ireland or Britain. At normal levels it covers well over two thousand hectares and holds a hundred and fifty million tonnes of water.

The creation of the reservoir was quite controversial at the time. It flooded seventy-six houses, fifty farms, an old church with a cemetery, a mill, a working turf bog, three bridges and several kilometres of road. The ESB acquired the property by compulsory purchase and, natu-

rally enough, most of the controversy centred around the amount of compensation they awarded the owners.

The rows reached the floor of the Dail and also prompted a Mr. R. Humphries BL to write an angry letter to the Leinster Leader. After ironically suggesting that it might be more humane if the Government were to machine gun the displaced people, he concluded…

> "…if the State is prepared to sink over a million pounds in a scheme for additional water for an already pampered Metropolis it can well afford to invest a few hundred thousand in the souls and bodies of the real martyrs of this cause – the unfortunate inhabitants of this doomed valley to whom this flooding of their homes comes as the very end of their world."

Eventually everything was sorted out and the lake began its gradual advance. The bodies were exhumed from the cemetery and re-buried with full clerical honours. There were frantic efforts to get the last loads of turf out of the bog and one stubborn householder was evacuated by boat when his floor was ankle deep in water. A post and wire perimeter fence was erected – it was over fifty km long.

From the outset it was envisaged that the new reservoir would not only provide water and electricity but also serve as a recreational amenity close to Dublin. This would include various boating activities and, in order to reduce the number of unpleasant shipwrecks, the taller structures needed to be demolished. At the time there were worries that we might be invaded (though there was some difference of opinion on which side in the war would be doing the invading) and it was thought that it would be a good idea to give our artillery forces a bit of target practice. Thus, killing two birds with one stone (or shell in this case), the Army was brought in, not to machine gun the inhabitants of the valley, but to demolish some of their houses after they'd left.

One of the wildlife highlights of the Blessington Lakes is its resident flock of greylag geese. The greylag is a large and musical species of wild goose which is the ancestor of all domestic goose breeds in the western world. It's thought that they bred in Ireland up until some time in the eighteenth century in the Bog of Allen and parts of Co. Down but then became extinct. However a small but growing number of the Icelandic breeding population visits this country every winter. The Blessington greylags are resident all year round but they are usually described with the rather derogatory adjective 'feral' – which means that they are tame birds that have gone wild. But it is not at all certain that the Blessington flock is composed entirely of escapees. Flocks of this nature have the ability to 'capture' wild birds

on migration. There is also the possibility that some of the genes may be from true domestic geese that have escaped from farmyards. Although domestic geese in this country are normally either white or a mixture of white and grey, and are often unable to fly, they very quickly revert to type if they get a chance go wild.

The Blessington Lakes flock of greylags roosts at night on the water. They fly out to graze on nearby fields during the day. So one of the best times to see the flock in the air, which is a spectacular sight, is at dawn or dusk when they're moving between the roosting site and the feeding site.

If you want to travel from the point where the Liffey enters the lake to the point where it leaves you have two choices – you can go clockwise, which is the long way round, or anti-clockwise. I'll start off by taking the longer road.

The Liffey meets the lake at a place called Three Castles. It's an old name, appearing in Irish in the Annals of the Four Masters. But it's also a bit of a mystery because today there's only one castle, in a reasonable state of repair, and no sign at all of the other two, or even any indication of where they stood. The castle (or castles) was a frontier post. In the late Middle Ages the uplands of the Wicklow and Dublin mountains were the stronghold of the O Tooles

*Greylags at Dawn
over Blessington
Lake*

and the O Byrnes, who were joined by people of many other clans who had lost their lands to the invading Anglo-Normans. They carried out ceaseless raids on the more fertile lowlands and the Anglo-Normans of the Pale had to build castles and garrison them to protect themselves.

There were several battles at Three Castles. One of them took place in 1538 and is mentioned in the State Papers of King Henry VIII. The forces of the crown were commanded by John Kelway, Constable of Rathmore, a strategic town on the hills to the west. He was pursued by the forces of Tirlagh O Toole and took refuge *'in a small pile called the Three Castles'*. But the O Tooles knew a thing or two about tackling castles and *'a thatched house adjoining to the same pile put afire, so that the head of the same pile, being covered with thatch and lacking battlement, took fire, and so all burned.'* Thatching a castle is obviously not a good idea.

The road south through the village of Oldcourt is a pleasant drive with views of the eastern shore of the lake. At various points you'll come across overgrown lanes or tracks leading down to the water. These are the remains of the old roads that were flooded when the dam was built. The new roads and the long concrete bridges that the ESB built to replace them amounted to a construction project nearly as difficult, expensive and time-consuming as the dams and power stations on the river.

Among the things that were inundated when the reservoir filled was St. Boden's Holy Well, a spring on the hillside below Lackan village. The well had many devotees who visited it to have their prayers answered and their illnesses cured. In 1978, nearly forty years after the well had disappeared, it reappeared again when the water in the reservoir fell to a record low level. The devotees petitioned the ESB who obligingly laid a pipeline up the hill from the spring and, above the maximum high water mark, installed a hand pump. They also donated a strip of their land to the friends of the well. A rectangular font carved out of a solid block of granite was placed under the pump and a little shrine built around it. Unfortunately we live in a more secular age and all this has recently disappeared.

Heading further south, you soon cross over a protrusion of the Wicklow granite near Ballyknockan. This is rather special rock. According to the Geological Survey it is: *'Rather fine-grained granite, nearly equal parts of felspar and quartz. Mica black. Quarried in joints and runs in an ENE direction'*. The result of this is that Ballyknockan has for centuries been a village of quarry men, stone masons and monumental sculptors.

The rather special rock has been sent all over Ireland and even abroad. The two stone lions that guard the portals of Stormont Castle on the outskirts of Belfast were born in Ballyknockan. There was a third one but apparently he was rejected, nobody seems quite sure why, and now he crouches, a little unfinished, on the roadside near the main quarry.

He wasn't the only commission that never left the place. The Virgin of Ballyknockan holds her Holy Child on a wayside track close to the village. She is weather-beaten and a little abandoned but still very beautiful. Presumably she was rejected by some Parish in favour of one of the painted plaster statues that were all the rage at the time. They made a mistake.

My own house, many old Irish miles to the west in Co. Kildare, has a fireplace and two massive nineteenth century gate-posts of Ballyknockan granite. I often wonder about the saga of transporting and erecting them in the days of horse power.

And the speckled rock can be admired in many of the cottages and cottage ruins in the area. Even the field boundaries contain fine stonework.

Cottage at Ballyknockan

Further to the south you can take a right turn up the peninsula on which the village of Valleymount stands and, continuing on, take a short cut to the western side of the lake across Humphrystown Bridge. But if you want to make the full circuit of the lake you should continue on southwards at the junction, heading for the King's River.

The village of Valleymount has an attractive small church with some fine examples of local stone carving in granite on the west front. It also has four beautiful windows by the stained-glass genius Harry Clarke. Three are memorials to named families but the fourth has a special dedication:

'Erected by the Quarry men of Ballyknockan in memory of their deceased parents and relatives.'

If you take the southern road to make the full circuit you will soon reach the bridge over the King's River, just above the point where it enters the lake. Here we must contemplate the appalling vista that this book is based on a false premise. The convention in geography is that when two rivers meet the stretch below the confluence takes the name of the larger of the two. Although I'm old, I'm not old enough to have actually seen the confluence of the King's River and the Liffey before it disappeared under the lake in 1940. But I have read accounts that suggest that the King's River was the larger one at this point.

I have examined maps and measured tributaries and catchment areas and it's hard to be conclusive. There doesn't seem to be much in it. But if my suspicions are correct then the noble stream that so obligingly separates southside Dubliners from their north-side brethren is not *Anna Livia*, it's the Kings River, and the title of this book is incorrect.

Shortly after crossing the bridge a right turn will take you on to the Baltyboys peninsula, a much larger one than the Valleymount peninsula. If you continue on across Burgage Bridge you'll intersect the main Dublin to Baltinglass road just south of Blessington village. This is, therefore, another short cut back to Three Castles where we started our circuit of the lake. About half way up the peninsula on the eastern side is the site of Blessington Sailing Club.

In May 1960 a small group of enthusiasts met in the Downshire Arms Hotel in Blessington and decided, by eight votes to six, to found a club and call it 'The Blessington Sailing Club', rather than the posher sounding 'Blessington Yacht Club'. They negotiated with the ESB and the County Council to get the site at Baltyboys but, due to their limited funds, the development of the site relied very much on unpaid voluntary work. Early on a number of members of the Defence Forces based in the Curragh joined the club, which was extremely fortunate because they turned out to have engineering skills and a well-developed work ethic. One of the first jobs was to build the access road in to the site and this is called 'The Burma Road' because it was built using officer labour.

If you continue on the full circuit of the lake, rather than taking the short cut over Burgage Bridge, the first place of real interest you come to is Poulaphouca and the dam.

This is not a big hydro scheme by international standards, or even by Irish ones. All the same, it was quite an achievement. At the height of construction there were three hundred men working on the dam plus a hundred and thirty building the bridges and roads and two hundred and fifty working on the water treatment plant and pipeline. Six lives were lost in work-place accidents.

The work started in 1937 and, although the dam was completed in 1940, the power stations didn't start full generation until 1947. The work took twice as long as it was supposed to because of the impact of the Second World War which made it difficult to commission and import things like turbines when all the large factories in Europe were concentrating on producing weapons and cargo ships were regularly being torpedoed.

At one point the war came very close to the construction project. One of the construction workers, Michael Murphy, was interviewed in the early 1990s and gave this dramatic account…

"I was taking the levels at the spillway at 4.25 am on the morning of 26th May 1941 when I saw two German planes coming up over Burke's Hotel. I could have sworn they were going to bomb the dam. They were coming in so low that you could see the swastikas on the wings. Five days later Dublin was bombed and people killed. I got a fierce fright. I was standing on a plank over the spillway taking the levels when they came over so low I could have hit them with a stick."

At the time it opened the Poulaphouca hydro Station was a major contributor to the electricity grid, its 38MW output capable of supplying over a third of the national requirement. Today due to the massive increase in demand for electricity, those same 38 MW would make up less than one percent of peak demand.

 But if the electric power provided by Blessington Lakes is rather less important than it was in 1947, the water supply is far more important. In fact, the growth in population in the Greater Dublin area and the development of thirsty new domestic appliances have made it absolutely vital.

There are several variant spellings of Poulaphouca but the name means the pool or the cavern of the pooka. The pooka is one of the most interesting bits of wildlife along the Liffey.

There is some disagreement among the experts about exactly what a pooka looks like but general agreement that it's a supernatural being that normally takes the form of an animal with a human face. The usual animal involved is a dog, though horse pookas are quite common and donkeys and goats are recorded. In Mary Chase's play *'Harvey'*,

'Horse Pooka?'

made into an Oscar-winning film in 1950, the pooka was a six foot three and a half inch tall white rabbit – but that, of course, was a work of fiction.

They seem to be confined to Ireland and Wales, though they probably had a wider distribution in earlier times. Puck from Shakespeare's *'A Mid-summer Night's Dream'* was a type of English pooka. I have recently discovered, and I think this may be rather significant, that 'puca' is also an old Irish word for *psilocybes*, or 'magic mushrooms'.

The pooka is occasionally malevolent but more commonly mischievous. The one at Poulaphouca was apparently a horse pooka and one of the mischievous things it did was to pick up people who were very drunk from the road side and take them for wild rides around the countryside before depositing them on their door steps. This must have been a most unpleasant experience for the drunks but at least it gave them a good excuse for the dishevelled state they arrived home in.

Anyway, before the dam was built the Liffey tumbled through a gorge at Poulaphouca in a series of three cataracts with a pool at the bottom of each. The place was popular with tourists in Victorian times – it was rather pretty and there was always the chance of spotting the pooka. The Blessington Steam Tram, an early ancestor of the Luas, connected Dublin and Blessington and in 1895 the line was extended to Poulaphouca to cater for the tourists. You can still see the little shop and ticket office of the terminal just to the north of the bridge. The service ended in 1927.

The bridge itself is quite spectacular, though unfortunately you can't get a really good view of it from the road and slithering down into the gorge is a bit dangerous. It was built in the 1820s by Alexander Nimmo and stands forty metres high with a span of twenty metres. It's made of blocks of sandstone finished in granite and the design concept was an enlightened one because it was intended to be beautiful as well as functional. So it's an early example of nineteenth century Mock-Gothic, with an arch like a church window and decorations of crosses, blind arches and turrets.

I'll come back to Poulaphouca in a while but, in the meantime, I'll have a look at the remaining bit of the western shoreline between here and Three Castles.

Russborough House is certainly the grandest of the grand houses in this part of the world – in fact some people think it's the finest Palladian mansion in Ireland. Building started in 1741 to the design of the renowned Richard Cassells (he was German and his surname is sometimes anglicised to Castle or Castles). It was commissioned by Joseph Lesson, first Earl of Milltown.

Sir Alfred Lane Beit, 2nd Baronet, who bought the house in 1952, was born in 1903 and went on to become, amongst other things, a British Conservative politician, a financier, a very serious art collector, a philanthropist and an honorary Irish citizen.

He married Clementine Mitford, a cousin of the famous Mitford sisters, and the couple spent some years deciding where they wanted to live. After the Second World War, during which he served in the RAF, he lost his seat in the House of Commons and became disillusioned with politics and the British Labour government so they went to live in South Africa. But there he became disillusioned with Apartheid so when his friend, Randal, Lord Dunsany, suggested he buy Russborough and come and live in Ireland he jumped at the chance. The price certainly wasn't a barrier because he had inherited most of the family fortune which had been made from diamond mines in South Africa.

The couple never had any children and devoted a lot of energy and money to charitable causes in Africa and Europe. They also collected old master painting and other art objects with taste, enthusiasm and a massive budget. They lived quietly at Russborough, supporting the Wexford Opera Festival and the fine arts in Ireland. In 1993 Sir Alfred was made an honorary Irish citizen in recognition, amongst other things, of his donation in 1987 of seventeen masterpieces to the National Gallery. At the time the gift was valued at a hundred million Irish pounds. It was described as '...*among the greatest single gifts to any gallery in the world in that generation...*' and a wing of the Merrion Square gallery was named after him.

The Beits were an incredibly generous couple but one motive for giving the pictures to the gallery was security. Russborough House may hold an international record for the number and frequency of art thefts from it. In 1974 an

IRA gang led by the English heiress Rose Dugdale broke into the house and pinched nineteen paintings, including a Goya, a Vermeer and a Gainsborough. The Beits, although they were elderly at this stage, were tied up and then needlessly pushed down a flight of stone stairs. In 1986 the house was robbed by the Dublin criminal Martin Cahill, more commonly known as 'The General'. He took eighteen paintings. In 2001 a Bellotto and a Gainsborough were stolen. In 2002 five paintings, including two by Rubens, were stolen in another robbery. Most of the paintings have been recovered.

Sir Alfred Beit died in 1994 and Lady Beit in 2005. There was a curious clause in her will stipulating that Sir Alfred's diaries should be kept secret until twenty-one years after the death of Queen Elizabeth II or seventy years after Lady Beit's own death. This caused some speculation that the diaries might contain material that would be embarrassing to the British royal family.

Russborough is now owned by a trust and is open to the public every day between May and September and on Sundays and bank holidays in April and October. Parties can visit by special arrangement at other times. Viewing is by guided tours only (they've had enough pilfering) and there's a shop and a café.

The history of the village of Blessington also contains elements of wealth, privilege and philanthropy. And there's something about the village that I've always liked. I think it has to do with the wide main street with its welcoming pubs which has a period feel to it. It was developed in the seventeenth century by an Archbishop of Dublin called Michael Boyle. He built the church in 1682 and soon afterwards provided it with a peal of six bells. The same bells, the original castings, are there to this day and are rung at six thirty every Saturday evening. The church clock also claims to be the oldest public clock in Ireland.

The Archbishop's estates were massive and they passed by marriage to the Hills family. Wills Hill ended a highly successful political career by becoming the first Marquis of Downshire in 1789. His title is commemorated in the Downshire Gallery, up until recently the Downshire Arms Hotel, and his inheritance included a mansion to the north-west of the village which was accidentally burned down at the end of the eighteenth century. The village itself was mostly burned down, and not accidentally, in the rising of 1798. Its current rather elegant appearance is the legacy of the 3rd Marquis, an extraordinary character who owned huge tracts of land spread over the whole island of Ireland.

Blessington Monument

The Marquis's correspondence, detailing the running of his various estates, amounts to thirty thousand letters and is kept in the Northern Ireland Public Records Office. The fountain opposite the church in Blessington has several very sycophantic inscriptions relating to the third Marquis. They read....

'A tribute of respect from the tenantry on the Wicklow, Kildare and Kilkenny estates of the Marquis of Downshire. Erected on the coming of age of the Earl of Hillsborough, 27th may 1853. The water supplied at the cost of a kind and generous landlord for the benefit of his attached and loyal tenants'.

It all sounds a little too good to be true but, contrary to what most of us have been taught, there were good landlords and grateful tenants in nineteenth century Ireland – as well as tyrants and rebels.

Travelling north, as we now are, you make a right turn in the middle of the main street in Blessington to take you back to the lake. At the bottom of the hill resist the temptation to turn right again over the last of the ESB bridges but continue on for a short and pleasant drive that brings you back to Three Castles and the point where we started our circumnavigation of the Blessington Lakes. The job is now done and we can return to the river at Poulaphouca.

The border between County Wicklow and County Kildare runs through Poulaphouca. This means that the Liffey will be Kildare's river until it reaches the sprawling suburbs of west Dublin

It also means that we have reached a significant point in the story. Up to now we have been dealing with the classic upper reaches of a river, even if part of that is today buried under the lake. We've seen the Liffey running fast and shallow down steep gradients, its water brown and acid. We have been in a landscape dominated by granite mountains covered in heather. But around the county boundary things change and we enter the more relaxed world of the middle reaches.

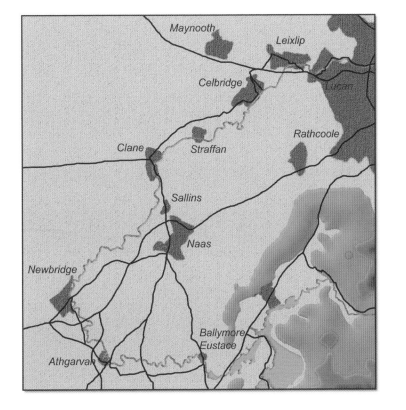

From the Poulaphouca dam the flow of the water is split. Some goes to the power station situated a little way down the valley on the other side of the road and some is piped down the hill to the treatment plant at Golden Falls. How the precious water is divided between the power station and the water treatment plant was a matter of concern from the very beginning. In 1936, before construction started, a strict agreement on this matter was drawn up and incorporated in an Act of the Oireachtas.

Once there was a succession of rapids and cascades on the river at this point but today there is a second dam at Golden Falls with a power station of its own. The ESB doesn't allow speed boats and craft that produce a large wash on the main Blessington Lakes which is a very good idea because fast boats can annoy nature lovers and slow boaters. However the same restriction does not apply to Golden Falls Lake which now has a water ski club on it. It is a good place to go if you think you might like to take up the sport as they give lessons and provide all the equipment at a reasonable price.

Below the dam the river takes a turn to the north, heading for Ballymore Eustace. The middle stretches of the Liffey in Co. Kildare are very attractive but unfortunately it's hard to get access to them except in towns and villages or at road bridges. The river flows through private property – farms and gardens, estates and studs – and if you try and explore on foot you'll be trespassing. But the people who own the banks don't actually own the river so if you travel by water you will not be breaking the law. This really means using a canoe, so this might be a good point to look at the Liffey as a canoeing river.

I've travelled most it by canoe and paddled the best bits many times. My preference is for an open Canadian canoe. This is partly because I once had an unpleasant experience when I borrowed a kayak that was too small for me and attempted to shoot a weir. I capsized and ended floating upside down with my head banging off the river bed, unable to either right the boat or get out of it. If an open Canadian capsizes you just fall out – and they have some other advantages too.

Water levels on the Liffey are unpredictable because they're controlled by the ESB. You can encounter a sudden flood, even in dry weather, if they open the sluices in one of the dams. But what's more likely to happen to you in summer and early autumn is that you'll find the river too shallow in places and your canoe will run aground on a weed bed or gravel bar. Then you have to get out and push, which is a much easier thing to do from a Canadian. I usually wear a pair of those shoes that scuba divers use made out of the same material as a wet suit, though in warm weather an old pair of canvas runners will do. If you try bare feet you'll discover that the stones can be surprisingly sharp!

The rapids in the river are pleasant rather than dangerous but some of the weirs can be very tricky in certain water conditions. You need to stop and inspect them before you decide whether to shoot them or portage past. The other common hazards on the faster parts of the river are what are called 'sweepers'. You come round a bend, travelling at speed, to find the way ahead blocked by a fallen tree. A common result, at least in my case, is that you end up scrabbling in the branches of the tree, looking like an anthropoid ape wearing a buoyancy aid, while your empty canoe continues on without you.

The Liffey is a long enough river to provide a leisurely camping cruise of several days duration. But this does involve sorting out camping spots in advance as there are no public camp grounds and you will almost certainly need a land-owner's permission. I don't think I've ever been refused.

Challenging times,
Liffey Descent

Another advantage of a Canadian, in my opinion, is that single paddles are extremely quiet and can be used in overgrown places where double paddles are awkward, particularly if you master the 'J-stroke'. The quietness means that you see a lot more of the river's wildlife. If this is important to you I'd recommend a canoe made of some form of plastic over an aluminium one.

Of course canoe cruising is only one form of the sport. There are also various kinds of competitive canoeing, most of which are Olympic disciplines. If this interests you there are about half a dozen canoe clubs along the river, including a large and well-equipped one on Leixlip reservoir. You'll also see slalom gates hanging over the water at several points, including upstream of the bridge in Newbridge and downstream of the bridge in Celbridge. The Irish Canoe Union is a good source of information.

Then, of course, there's the Liffey Descent. This internationally famous downhill canoe race is held every September on a thirty kilometre course between Straffan and Islandbridge. It involves ten weirs, two sets of rapids and a long and punishing portage round the dam in Leixlip. The ESB adds to the fun by releasing thirty million tons of water to create a massive flood. It is way beyond my paddling competence but I enjoy it as a spectator.

Whether you arrive in Ballymore Eustace by canoe or by road, be sure to admire the lovely old six-arched masonry bridge over the river. Before Nimmo's Bridge at Poulaphouca was built in the 1820s this was the main road bridge connecting Dublin to Baltinglass and points south. Afterwards the village tended to be bye-passed and declined somewhat in size and importance.

The 'Eustace' bit of the name refers to a family with that surname who came over with the Norman conquest and were important land-owners in the area for several centuries. Today the village sprawls in a slightly confusing manner up the flank of the hill above the river. It has a large square, several good pubs, an old church with a rather fine interior and some old grave-stones and a ruined mill. I'll discuss the water mills on the Liffey when we get a bit further down-stream.

One of the most fascinating and beautiful wild animals found in the middle reaches is the otter. The majority of Irish people have never seen an otter in the wild and yet, after our three species of deer, they are our largest wild land animal. Males, or dog otters, average eleven kilos and can reach sixteen. Females are smaller, about seven kilos. And they are not that rare. The species found in Ireland is called the Eurasian otter and we have the highest population density of them in western Europe.

Casting near
The Old Mill at
Ballymore Eustace

Despite this they're not the easiest of animals to see and there are several reasons for this. The first one is that they're largely nocturnal although in very cold weather otters will fish in the afternoons when the water temperature is higher than at night and in mid-summer they will be active after dawn and before dusk because the nights are too short for them to catch enough food during the hours of darkness.

Another reason is that you won't find high concentrations of otters in any one place because the males are strictly territorial and the territories are quite large. An otter territory on the Liffey will consist of several kilometres of river and the male who holds it will not allow any other males on this stretch.

Naturally shy creatures they, like all members of the weasel family, have a powerful sense of curiosity and this sometimes overcomes their timidity. I have sat quietly in a small boat while, diving and surfacing again, a dog otter inspected me at close range for about fifteen minutes.

The Liffey's otter population is of international conservation importance because the species is extinct or threatened over much of its natural range. Its future depends on three things – unpolluted water, plenty of fish and control

Otter

of building development along the banks of the middle reaches of the river.

The Liffey has now grown to be a considerable river and the stretch between Ballymore Eustace through Harristown to Kilcullen is very attractive. It meanders between stands of mature trees, the water is clear and shallow, flowing over brown gravel with many long clumps of Ranunculus or Water Crowfoot. This is actually a relation of the buttercup that grows in streams and rivers, its flowers appear in May and June and have white petals with a yellow centre. But unless you have a canoe you will not be able to enjoy any of this because there is no public access to this stretch.

You will have to make do with glimpses of the river from high above on the road. Paradoxically far fewer people actually get a good view of this stretch of river than enjoy the 'wilderness' stretch just below the source.

The situation with regard to public access to the Irish countryside in general is very unsatisfactory. A generation ago the question hardly ever arose. If you wanted to walk across a farmer's field to pick mushrooms, watch birds, or just to get to something on the other side, there were no objections. And people who did this kind of thing were careful to close gates, not let their dog chase livestock and replace a stone accidentally knocked off a bank. But today our society is less open and welcoming, more litigious and money-conscious. Every year increasing amounts of our countryside, even open mountain side, become off-limits. And it's not only Irish countryside lovers who are suffering. Tourism by ramblers and walkers is a big growth industry in most countries but is declining here.

The situation in other countries is different. In many of them a citizen has a constitutional right to walk anywhere and this is only restricted in certain very specific circumstances. In countries where there is no such constitutional 'right to roam' there is usually a dense network of public rights of way, bridle-paths and long distance walking routes that are guaranteed by law. We don't benefit from either of these two models.

There have been attempts to do something about this but meetings between farming organisations and groups lobbying for the rights of walkers and countryside lovers have dragged on for years with little real progress and increasingly rural beauty is something we have to enjoy vicariously from the sanctuary of the public road.

And the public road next meets the Liffey at the lovely stone bridge at Harristown, a strong contender when I try to decide on my favourite bridge across the river. There is an inscription on the bridge that states, in rather uneven lettering, that it was built in 1788 by 'Ino LaTouche'. His stately home, Harristown House, looks down on the river from the north bank. There is a grove of fine old beech trees at the bridge and at one time you could walk for quite a way along the river bank here, using a path with stiles constructed by a local angling club. In line with the trend, this access seems to have gone in recent times. If you continue on by road you pass through the pretty village of Brannockstown with its tiny Baptist church.

Thankfully the good people of Kilcullen have opened up a riverside park and walkway so there is, at last, a bit of public access. And the river here is attractive, quite fast after it passes under the tall spans of the bridge – fast enough to support a canoe club and fast enough to capsize me once, many years ago. The bridge carries a fair bit of traffic, though not as much as it did in the days before the motorway passed the outskirts of the village. It was widened at some time in the past. The downstream side is the original limestone, five-arched structure. On the upstream side the bridge was widened using reinforced concrete but it was done sensitively and faced with cut stone.

Near the top of the hill in the main part of the park is Saint Brigid's Holy Well with a relief sculpture of the saint feeding the poor done by Father Flanagan of Newbridge College. Below this a stile marks the start of an ancient footpath to a cemetery. Hidden among the modern gravestones and monuments are some older ones. Fragments of three or four tombs have been fixed together to make a low wall. One fragment dates from before 1550 and shows Saint Catherine with her wheel, the Virgin and Child and another female saint who's hard to identify. Close by, but also hard to find, is the recumbent stone image of Roland Eustace, Baron Portlester, and his Lady. He founded a monastery on this site and the place is still known as Newabbey, although he died in 1495. Some bits of the abbey have been cemented into the cemetery wall. The baron who founded it was a descendent of the Eustace who founded Ballymore nearly two centuries earlier.

The attractive main street of Kilcullen village rises steeply from the bridge. Among its attractions are a bookshop with a café, a wonderful traditional cobbler and shoemaker, a saddler and one of the finest butcher's shops in Ireland. If you continue on you'll come to an even more interesting graveyard and a more ancient monastic settlement in Old Kilcullen. It dates back to the fifth century. There are the remains of a round tower but the chief item of interest is a damaged High Cross.

There's some dispute among scholars about the exact age of High Crosses but they certainly date from either the eighth or ninth century. Along with manuscripts like the Book of Kells and the Book of Durrow, they are examples of the huge contribution Ireland made to western European art in this period. It's thought that the stone crosses had wood and metal precursors, though no large examples survive. They are carved in relief with biblical scenes, almost like cartoons in a stone comic book. It's suggested that these were used by priests or monks to teach scripture to illiterate people, though they almost certainly had other ritual functions as well.

The High Cross in Old Kilcullen is not the best preserved example in the country but it's the only one in the Liffey valley. Some of the images are a bit hard to decipher but apparently the east side of the shaft has the twelve Apos-

Ancient Monastic

settlement, Old

Kilcullen

tles divided between three panels. The north side shows the man who would become King David confronting a lion, some decorative interlace and a Bishop, believed to be Saint Mac Tail, smiting something or someone with his crozier. The south side is mostly decorative and the top panel is a human interlace. The west side of the shaft is the best bit. Here we have Samson slaying another lion, a horseman blowing a trumpet and some people with a donkey. The donkey is wonderful because its ears are longer than its legs. Some experts say the donkey relief is about the flight into Egypt, others that it's Christ's entry into Jerusalem.

To the west of Old Kilcullen is Dun Ailinne, also known as Knockaulin, a large, green flat-topped mound that was the seat of the kings of Leinster in the Iron Age before Saint Patrick arrived here and founded the monastery that was later to be run by Saint Mac Tail. Actually Dun Ailinne has a very long habitation history that stretches back into the Bronze Age and forwards into historical times. It was finally abandoned in the eighteenth century when people felt secure enough to come down from a high and windy hill top and live in more sheltered spots.

The significance of Dun Ailinne comes from the fact that it overlooks the Curragh of Kildare, which seems to have been a very important place in Leinster from the earliest

times. Part of the difficulty in writing a book like this is deciding how wide a corridor a river has. There's an argument that says that the Curragh comes close to the Liffey but doesn't actually reach its banks and so it should be excluded. But it used to be called 'Cuirrech Life', or the Curragh of the Liffey, before it was called the Curragh of Kildare and it's so intimately bound to the history, hydrology, culture and industry of the Liffey valley that I've decided to let it in.

So, what is the Curragh? It's a three and a half thousand hectare plain of alluvial gravel that avoided division during the enclosures of the eighteenth and nineteenth centuries and remains an open grass sward dotted with clumps of furze. The gravel is up to seventy metres deep and very free-draining so there's no natural standing water. This makes it unsuitable for cattle but it is grazed by sheep which don't need to drink because they get enough moisture from eating grass. But above all the Curragh belongs to thoroughbred horses and strings of them are exercised and trained on it every morning.

The history of horse racing on the Curragh is long and interesting. In prehistoric times the Kings of Leinster used to hold an important event called 'The Fair of the Liffey' on the Curragh. We don't know a lot about it but it seems to have involved a combination of oaths of loyalty to the

*Early morning
Gallop on the
Curragh*

king from lesser chieftains and competitive sports, with horse racing as the centre piece. Later on, around 600AD, a poem was written describing how, a century before, Saint Brigid had enjoyed driving her chariot drawn by two horses over the Curragh, which she probably owned at the time. There's no indication that Brigid actually raced chariots competitively but some of her successors certainly did. The Abbot Cobhthach was known as 'Racing Cobhthach' and his passion for fast horses survives among some Kildare clergy to this day.

Modern horse racing on the Curragh developed in the seventeenth century among members of the aristocracy laying bets that they had faster horses than their neighbours. For example in 1634 Lord Digby and the Earl of Ormond matched each other's horses over four miles on the Curragh. In the following century there was a famous race on the Curragh between 'Black and All Black' and 'Bajazet'

St. Bridgits Chariot

for a huge purse of one thousand guineas, with about ten times that amount in side-bets. 'Black and All Black' won, which resulted in a duel. This not only established the tradition of giving

race horses silly names, it also ensured that the Curragh became the centre for the Liffey valley's massive blood-stock industry. Today one of the highest concentrations of quality race horses in the world is found along the banks of the river in County Kildare.

The Curragh lies between the towns of Newbridge and Kildare and today it is, somewhat controversially, bisected by a motorway. For much of the distance between the two towns the motorway is in a cutting below ground level. The main reason for doing this was to avoid the danger of the traffic frightening the horses in the Irish National Stud. That's how important horses are in this part of Kildare.

But back to the river itself which, after it leaves Kilcullen, heads for Athgarvan. The word 'ath' occurs commonly in Irish place names and means a ford. The river here is quite broad and shallow and suitable for fording in the days before the bridge was built. There is a local tradition that one of the five great roads that radiated out from Tara in ancient times crossed the Liffey here. But the river looks a bit different to what it must have been like in those days because there is now a long weir upstream of the bridge that impounds water that used to power another water-mill. The ruins of the mill and the chimneys of a malt

Bridge at
Athgarvan

house are still there and it is possible to walk for a short way along the bank and have a look around.

If you're travelling by road from Kilcullen to Athgarvan just before you reach the bridge you'll pass a curious mound covered in trees and scrub. This is a man-made structure called Rosetown Rath. Not much is known about it and I can find no record of archaeological work done here. My own guess is that there was originally an ancient rath or ring fort here but that the Normans modified it to make a motte and bailey type castle to control the strategic river crossing.

Raths are interesting things and quite a lot of them survive all over the country, including along the banks of the Liffey. But, despite the fact that they occur at a density of something like one every two square kilometres in the countryside, there is surprisingly little consensus among scholars about what they were for or even when they were built. The lack of definitive answers allows lay people the freedom to speculate.

They are sometimes called 'Fairy Forts' but I am very dubious about the supernatural explanation of their origin. My own view is that the banks were originally reinforced by cut thorn branches and the space inside, it's called the 'vallum', was principally to protect livestock from wild animals

at night. Sometimes people lived inside with the animals and sometimes they didn't. Raths were in use at a time before there were enclosed fields in Ireland and the farmers were pastoralists who followed their herds through the open countryside, brandishing weapons at any predatory animal that had the temerity to turn up in daylight. At night they shut the livestock up in the rath for safe-keeping. It's interesting that some experts believe that raths were in use in more remote parts of the Irish countryside until the eighteenth century. This century is significant for two things – it sees the extinction of the wolf in Ireland and the start of large scale field enclosure.

After Athgarvan the river flows to meet the largest town so far, Newbridge.

Some sources claim that the history of the town only starts in 1819. In fact there has been a settlement at this important fording point on the river for thousands of years – and the original 'new bridge' was built as early as 1308 at a spot a couple of hundred metres upstream of the current bridge. Today's bridge dates from 1936 but in 2006 it was extensively, and tastefully, refurbished and widened to include a pedestrian boardwalk on each side. The significance of 1816 is that it was the date that the British Army established a cavalry barracks in the town, causing it to grow and prosper. They were attracted by two things

Droichead Nua at
Newbridge

– the grasslands of the Curragh and the water of the Liffey. There were a thousand men and about the same number of horses billeted here and a thousand horses drink a lot. They were led out from the barracks through the 'watering gates', which have now disappeared, to quench their thirst from the Liffey. At one time this was home to the 11th Hussars under the command of the man who would become Lord Cardigan. They took part in the notorious 'Charge of the Light Brigade' in the Crimea in 1843. Not much is left of the original barracks today, though some of it is incorporated in the Bord na Mona headquarters behind the Post Office. The Garrison Church became the Town Hall and today contains FAS offices, though I believe another change of use is planned for the near future.

There is much good town planning in modern Newbridge and this includes an excellent park called 'The Strand' with riverside walks and a nature trail with explanatory signs. The Riverbank Arts Centre is a pleasant modern building with a café as well as a theatre and gallery space. It was a Millennium Project, though it didn't become fully functional until a couple of years into the century. This part of the east midlands has a particularly strong tradition of amateur drama. There are other connections with the arts. If you walk downstream from the bridge you'll come to Newbridge College, founded by the Dominicans in 1852. It has a small modern church which not only has good stained glass it also has examples of the sculpture of Father Henry Flanagan OP who lived from 1918 to 1992 and was a teacher in the school. We first came across his work in Kilcullen and, as well as sculpting in various materials, he was extremely gifted musically. Another famous native was Molly Keane who was born in Ryston Lodge on the outskirts of Newbridge and not, as is often claimed, in County Wexford.

The Liffey has a very healthy population of kingfishers and the new bridge in Newbridge is one of the most convenient places to watch them. They sometimes actually land on the bridge, despite all the traffic, but at other times they fish from overhanging branches upstream of the bridge on the Dublin rather than the town side of the river.

Kingfishers must have the most exotic plumage of any Irish bird. They really look as though they belong in a tropical rainforest rather than on the banks of a river like the Liffey. Their back is a metallic cobalt colour and this is tinged with green on the head and wings. The under-parts and ear coverts are a shining chestnut and the chin and sides of the neck are white. The beak is black and orange and the legs are bright red. These are really the colours of a gaudy butterfly rather than a bird.

Early morning stroll, 'Strand' at Newbridge

Kingfisher

I suspect that the majority of Irish people have never actually seen a kingfisher in the wild. The exceptions would be anglers, boaters and river lovers. But the birds are actually quite widely distributed around the country, except in the northwest. David Cabot's 'Irish Birds' gives an estimate of between thirteen hundred and two thousand one hundred breeding pairs in the country and notes that numbers are declining. I'm not sure of the accuracy of this. Kingfishers are not easy to count and, though there's little doubt that they're declining in numbers over most of their European range, my own observations suggest that numbers have increased in Ireland over the past twenty years.

Kingfishers are territorial and seldom travel long distances, except in very hard winters when their fishing grounds freeze over. They nest in burrows in river banks. The burrows are about a metre long and end in a nest chamber. The birds usually excavate them themselves with their formidable beaks but have been known to take over disused rat holes or sand martin burrows. At the end of the burrow these beautiful things construct what may well be the most disgusting nest in the whole bird world. It's made from left-over bits of fish – heads, tails, fins and so on – plus pellets of scales and bones vomited up by the birds. All this rapidly starts to decompose with the result that kingfisher eggs, which are almost perfectly round and pinkish white when they're laid, rapidly become stained an evil greenish brown.

They feed by waiting on a perch, usually a tree branch hanging over the river, and then diving on their prey. They can penetrate the water for a depth of at least a metre and have eyes specially adapted to seeing accurately in both air and water. I have occasionally seen them fishing off bridges and even tall reeds, though reeds tend to sway too much in the wind to giver them an accurate shot. The main item in their diet is, obviously, small fish. On the Liffey they eat a lot of minnows and seldom tackle anything much larger. But they also eat quite a lot of large invertebrates and sometimes gorge on *gammarus*, the freshwater shrimp, which is only about the size of a little fingernail.

There is an ancient classical legend that tells the story of the first kingfishers, or halcyons as they used to be called. It's quite a long story, but this is the gist of it. Halcyone was a beautiful Princess who lived on an island in the Mediterranean. Her father was Aelus, King of the Winds, and she had four brothers. They were Boreas, the north wind, Zephyrus the west wind, Auster the south wind and Eurus the east wind. Aelus was a nice old man but he found his sons hard to control. They were headstrong lads with a cruel streak and were forever slipping off and creating terrible storms at sea, causing ships to sink and sailors to drown.

One day Ceyx, the handsome young King of Thessaly, visited the island. Ceyx and Halcyone fell in love with each other and eventually Aelus gave them permission to marry. Halcyone's four brothers were very annoyed about this but they couldn't prevent Ceyx and Halcyone from sailing back to Thessaly as man and wife.

The royal couple were very happy together but one day Ceyx announced that he had to sail off on a business trip. Halcyone wasn't keen on this and tried to persuade him to cancel the trip but he refused. Then she tried to persuade

him to take her along but he wouldn't do that either and eventually he sailed off over the horizon, leaving her behind.

Her worst fears were realized when her brothers slipped away from their father and got their own back on Ceyx for stealing their sister by creating an almighty storm in which the royal ship sank and Ceyx was drowned. Halcyone learnt the news in a dream and, broken-hearted, went down to the harbour. Here she spotted her husband's corpse washing up in the waves. She was about to fling herself off the harbour wall in despair when she unexpectedly sprouted a pair of wings and turned into the world's first kingfisher. So she flew down and kissed her dead husband with her new beak. He then came back to life and turned into another kingfisher and they flew off together over the sea.

After a while they decided the world could use a few more kingfishers so they constructed a cunning floating nest woven out of fish bones in which Halcyone laid a clutch of eggs. Aelus knew what was going on and he had been really cross about what his sons had done. So he made quite sure that all four of them were confined to barracks until the eggs hatched and the baby kingfishers were reared. And that's why the expression 'halcyon days' means an extended period of peace and calm.

Himalayan Balsam

The Liffey flows over the weir at the foot of the College lawns and leaves Newbridge. It passes, in turn, a halting site for the travelling community, a big house and a cemetery with a Holy Well. Then it arrives at a charming spot with an amazing name. At Morristown Lattin there is some public access to the river above Victoria Bridge. The banks are lined by fine mature trees, mainly beeches with large willows and alders, and the river runs at some pace in a number of channels and over a semi-derelict weir that feeds a mill-race. Many wild flower species, plus the naturalized Himalayan Balsam, add to the attractions of the spot in their season.

The mill itself is a rather magnificent eighteenth century flour mill on the site of a much older corn mill. A former owner, the artist Eoin O Toole, restored it to full working order in the 1990s and converted the interior into a dwelling. I met him at the time and I have eaten bread baked from flour ground by the massive breast-shot wheel, which is over four metres in diameter. Vertical water wheels are either over-shot, under-shot or breast-shot, depending on whether the water flows over the top of them, underneath them or strikes them half way up.

It's easy to forget how important water power was to industry in this country before the introduction of the steam engine. In fact even after the introduction of steam it had many economic advantages. It was really the widespread availability of electricity in the middle of the last century that signalled the final end of the water mills. It's ironic that the electricity generated by the turbines of the Liffey Scheme killed off the river's mills.

It's not quite clear when the notion of using the power of falling water to take the labour out of grinding grain was first discovered. The Ancient Greeks were certainly doing it in the first century BC and the Han Dynasty Chinese some time before that – though these were separate discoveries. In Ireland there were small water mills associated with monastic sites in the Early Christian Period and some massive ones associated with the medieval monasteries of the great continental religious orders.

The huge mill further down the river at Islandbridge has a typical history. It was established in the Middle Ages by a very wealthy and powerful religious order called the Knights of Saint John of Jerusalem. But it appears they

Restored Mill Wheel
at Morristown Lattin

built on the site of a much older mill associated with Saint Maighnenn who was an Abbot and Bishop who lived around 650 AD and gave his name to Kilmainham.

Nearly two hundred mill sites have been identified on the Liffey and its tributaries. Originally these would have been corn mills. Local farmers brought their grain in to the miller who ground it and returned it to them as a coarse grist in exchange for a small payment in cash or kind. This was a vital operation in the Middle Ages because, before the introduction of the potato, bread was central to everyone's diet.

Flour mills like the one at Morristown Lattin first appeared on the Liffey about 1760. They tended to operate on a more capitalist basis. The miller bought grain from farmers over a much wider area, ground it into a variety of fine flours and then re-sold them to bakeries and retail outlets. Most mills produced both wheaten and oaten meals.

But the Liffey's mills ended up doing far more than just grinding grain. We know that the river and its tributaries also had paper mills, cotton and calico printing mills, oil mills, gun-powder mills, woollen mills and saw-mills.

The oil mills crushed linseed, the seeds of the flax plant, to extract linseed oil. This was a vital product before the widespread availability of mineral oils and was used in a variety of domestic and industrial processes. The 'cake' left after the oil was extracted was normally used in livestock feeds. The gunpowder mills were dangerous affairs because they produced what was called 'black powder', a much more volatile explosive than modern gun-powder. It was made by mixing ground up charcoal, sulphur and saltpetre, which is potassium nitrate. The best charcoal for the job was apparently made from alder wood, which would have been convenient for the water mills because alders in this country grow almost exclusively on the banks of rivers and the shores of lakes. But the mills had such a strong tendency to explode violently, causing much damage and loss of life, that they were all small and situated well away from each other and, as much as possible, away from human habitation.

Victoria Bridge has two wide arches of cut limestone and was completed in 1837, the date of the Coronation of the young Queen Victoria. The river flows through it and through the townland of Yeomanstown to the next crossing point on the outskirts of Carragh village. This bridge is old and very narrow, only allowing one line of traffic at a time. It's supported by six stone piers with round-headed arches and the stone-work is rough and rustic compared to the nineteenth century sophistication of Victoria Bridge. I like old bridges and this is another of my Liffey favour-

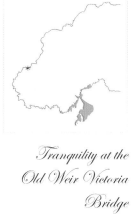

Tranquility at the Old Weir Victoria Bridge

ites. The river is attractive here too, quite fast-flowing with some good trout fishing.

If you're travelling by road the next point with access to the river is the Leinster Aqueduct near Sallins. This is a truly magnificent piece of late eighteenth century engineering that carries the Grand Canal and a road across the river. Originally the plan was that canal boats would lock down into the river, cross it and lock back up into the canal on the other side and teams of labourers began to dig the locks. But then a much bolder plan was developed that dispensed with locks and carried the canal over the river at a height of eight metres on one level using an aqueduct. The aqueduct is made of cut limestone and was completed in 1780. There is some public access around it and you can actually cross under the canal and road using a 'dry arch' at the western end of the aqueduct. The dry arch is usually far from dry and you may need wellies but the vaulting above your head is decorated with miniature stalactites formed from the calcite leached out of the limestone by centuries of seepage from the canal.

The traditional name for the towpath on the Grand Canal is 'the horse-walk'. Today it is also a long distance public walkway. The walk out from Sallins on the north bank of the canal to the aqueduct is popular and pleasant, though to approach it from Digby Bridge to the west is even nicer.

At the eastern end of the aqueduct is a pump house and three blue-painted pipes connecting the river to the canal. One of the problems with canals is keeping them fed with enough water in times of drought. The principal water source for the Grand Canal is Pollardstown Fen where water from the Curragh aquifer erupts in a series of springs. But even this wonderful source is sometimes unable to cope with the demand from the canal and then water from the Liffey is pumped up at the aqueduct to help out.

The river flows under the aqueduct and next meets the road at another attractive bridge at Millicent. There is no real public access here but the bridge has two 'pedestrian refuges' in the centre where you can linger in safety and admire this pretty stretch of water. There are also some fine old trees in the area, mostly beeches and limes. Unfortunately the two largest beeches have fallen in recent years. Beeches are not particularly long-lived for a large deciduous species. After about two hundred and fifty years they become, to use the technical forestry term 'senile' and riddled by fungi. They are also not a native Irish species, though they are native to a small part of southern England. In the 1750s and 60s it was fashionable for larger landowners to plant both beech and lime. These beeches are now all senile, though the limes are still vigorous and healthy.

A passage in time
- Leinster Aquaduct
- Sallins

We don't know the life-expectancy of the limes because they're hybrids and the hybrid has only been available in any quantity for about three hundred years. So we'll have to wait to see how long it lives and we may have to wait a very long time. The two parents of the hybrid, the small-leaved lime and the broad-leaved lime, are very long-lived trees indeed. They are both rather rare natives of England and parts of Wales, though not of Ireland, and archaeologists in England have found a living grove of the small-leaved species that appears to pre-date an early Viking settlement. This would give the trees a minimum age of twelve hundred years.

Not far from the bridge at Millicent is the Church of Ireland Church of St. Michael and All Angels. It is a magnificent example of Victorian architecture. Unfortunately most of the magnificence is on the inside and the Church is normally locked. If you want to admire the interior with its Italianate tile mosaics you will have to contact the Rector or attend a service. But one of the interesting exterior points is the English-style lych gate with its slate roof under which a coffin would be placed before burial.

After Millicent the Liffey meanders, as it so often does in Co. Kildare, through large stud farms. One of them, Blackhall Stud, belongs to Sheikh Maktoum, ruler of Dubai and the biggest player in the horse racing world. It also passes close to Bodenstown graveyard, where Wolfe Tone is buried. Then it flows over a small weir and under Alexandra Bridge on the outskirts of Clane. The bridge was built in 1864 and named after Princess Alexandra who the year before had married the Prince of Wales, later to become King Edward VII. The bridge builders on the Liffey seem to have had Royalist sympathies.

Before the bridge there was a ford and the ford seems to have had strategic significance from very early times. Close to the fording spot is the Mound of Clane, traditionally the burial place of Mesgegra, King of Leinster, who was killed in single combat with the Ulster warrior Conal Cernagh of the Red Branch Knights. It was the culmination of a complicated quarrel recorded in the Book of Leinster and, even more long-windedly, in a poem by Sir Samuel Ferguson.

There is some pleasant public access to the river bank in front of the Abbey. Clane Abbey was founded by Gerald FitzMaurice, Lord of Offaly, and building began in 1260. The Church and Friary were once rather magnificent, even in ruins. But Clane has seen very rapid development in recent years and what remains of the Lord of Offaly's great project is now surrounded by a shopping mall, apartment blocks and a hotel. The complex is called 'Abbeylands'.

There are an amazing number of abbey ruins along the course of the Liffey. When the great continental religious orders arrived in Ireland in the Middle Ages (the first ones came well before the Norman invasion of Ireland at the end of the twelfth century) they occasionally founded their abbeys on the site of a monastery of the Celtic Church. But some of them were founded on 'green field' sites and they had a preference for river banks. This was partly because the abbeys were large-scale agricultural enterprises and the monks had the capital and skills to build water mills to grind the corn that was the staple crop in medieval agriculture. But it was also because they had an extremely strict dietary regime that involved frequent fast days on which they ate fish. The wild fish, particularly salmon, trout and eels, which were plentiful in Irish rivers at the time supplied part of their requirements. But they were also skilful fish farmers and used the river water to supply stew ponds in which they bred and reared a wide variety of other fish species to be used when the wild fish were scarce or unavailable. Some of these fish were imported from Britain or the continent and it's believed that many Irish coarse fish species originated as escapees from monastic stew ponds.

After it leaves Clane the Liffey meanders through rich farmland, much of it arable, and the banks are lined by tall willows. It's heading for Straffan but, just before it reaches the village, it enters the rather dramatic landscape of the grounds of the K Club. This luxurious country club, with two golf courses, a fishery, a five star hotel and a spa, is internationally famous because it was the venue for the Ryder Cup in 2006. But the estate actually has a long history.

In fact the club claims that the history of the estate and Straffan House, which now forms the main part of the hotel, goes back to 550 AD. I imagine that American visitors find this quite impressive but in fact historical detail before the Norman Conquest is a bit vague. But there is no doubt that Strongbow granted the lands to Maurice Fitzgerald at the end of the twelfth century. Maurice's eldest son passed it on to his younger brother Gerald, who was an ancestor of the Duke of Leinster. King John of England, the man who signed the Magna Carta in 1215, confirmed this grant some time afterwards.

The estate then remained in the hands of a series of wealthy families, most of them titled, until the middle of the twentieth century. In the sixteenth century it belonged to the de Penkistons but they chose the wrong side in a rebellion and forfeited it. Then the Gaydon family took it over but something similar happened to them in the following century when Cromwell arrived and they forfeited it to the Bewleys. But eventually the Gaydons were found innocent of the charges against them and got back seven hundred acres which, in 1679, they sold to Richard Talbot for £700. Property prices in the Straffan area have increased considerably since then. It's now one of the most expensive places in Ireland to live.

Perhaps the most interesting family to own the place that's now the K Club during its long and chequered history was the Bartons. Hugh Barton purchased the property in 1831. He was a descendent of one of the 'Wild Geese' and his family had lived in western France for many generations and made a fortune out of the wine business. There were many such families, like the Lynchs, the O Briens, the Hennessys, the MacMahons, whose names, sometimes altered to be more French, are now connected with famous chateaux wines and brandies from the Bordeaux area. The O Briens gave their name to Chateau Haut Brion and the Barton name is still alive in the well-known brand of Barton et Guestier.

But the Bartons were forced out of France during the infamous 'Reign of Terror' following the French Revolution and eventually ended up ploughing all their fortune into building a French style chateau on the banks of the Liffey outside Straffan. This house is now the east wing of the modern hotel. Building started in 1832 and while it was

going on the Bartons lived in nearby Barberstown Castle, which today is also a hotel.

The design was based on the chateau at Louveciennes, to the west of Paris. But Hugh Barton was not totally consistent in his architectural tastes and later added an Italian style campanile, which is still there. The whole thing was rounded off by some truly magnificent landscape gardening. He lived happily in the house with his wife Anne to the ripe old age of eighty-nine and the two of them are buried in the Church of Ireland graveyard in Straffan. The house and estate remained in the possession of the Barton family until 1949.

The house then passed into the hands of a succession of colourful characters including Steven O Flaherty, Kevin McClory, an Iranian general, Patrick Gallagher and the Ferguson family. The Jefferson Smurfit Group, one of the world's largest paper and packaging companies, bought it in 1988. The K Club opened as a resort in 1991. In 2005 Dr. Michael Smurfit and Mr. Gerry Gannon, as private individuals, bought the resort from the company. Today it is an icon of luxurious leisure and the buildings and grounds are still magnificent.

At the bridge in Straffan the Liffey flows over quite a high weir and between two churches before it enters the pretty

*Mirrors of time by the
K-Club, Straffan*

little village. There are a number of visitor attractions, including the Guinness Steam Museum, a must for anyone with an interest in industrial archaeology, and an excellent butterfly farm. The butterfly farm, run by enthusiasts Des and Iris Fox, is open to the public during the summer and its tropical houses will interest gardeners as well as lepidopterists.

After Straffan the Liffey flows to the north of Lyon's Hill. The hill has a slightly artificial look to it and this is not deceptive because it is actually Liamhuin, one of several royal seats of the Kings of Leinster, and crowned by earthworks that go back at least to the Iron Age. Like Dun Ailinne near Kilcullen it is a strategic high point surrounded by exceptionally fertile land.

Lyon's Hill is also one of the places claimed to be the site of the duel between Daniel O Connell and John d'Esterre in February 1815. The mansion on the flank of the hill is Lyon's House, built in 1797 for Lord Cloncurry. In 1962 it became part of the Faculty of Agriculture of University College Dublin. Today it belongs to the businessman Tony Ryan. An on-going development which is well worth a visit is the restoration of the 'Lyon's Village' on the canal bank. It contains, among other attractions, a gourmet restaurant and an informal café-restaurant under the direction of the Irish celebrity chef, Richard Corrigan.

After the Lyon's estate and the rather scattered village of Ardclough the Liffey approaches Celbridge. Today it's a busy, bustling commuter town but the centre contains several buildings of historical interest.

Celbridge Abbey is somewhat unusual because it actually is a functioning abbey today. It was bought by the Saint John of God Brothers, in a state of some dereliction, in 1952. They restored it and use it to carry on the traditional mission of the Order, which is caring for the sick and people with special needs. But it was originally a grand private house, built in the 1690s by a wealthy Dutchman, Bartholomew van Homrigh, who was Lord Mayor of Dublin. It was extensively re-designed at the end of the eighteenth century by Dr. Richard Marley, who was Henry Grattan's uncle. Grattan wrote many of his most famous speeches here. Part of the grounds are open to the public (check opening times and entrance charges) and include gardens, pleasant river-side walks, a café and shop and a rare and magnificent specimen of an Oriental Plane tree. But the gardens and the river-side walk are most famous for their connection with the strange love life of Dr. Jonathan Swift.

When Swift was living in London he met the daughter of the man who built the house in Celbridge. Her name was Esther van Homrigh (sometimes Hester Vanhomrigh) but

Lovers' retreat,
Celbridge Abbey

posterity knows her as 'Vanessa', the name Swift gave her in his letters and verses. They appear to have fallen in love, though there was a considerable age difference.....

'Vanessa, not in years a score,
Dreams of a gown of forty-four,
Imaginary charms can find
In eyes with reading almost blind.'

Swift moved to Dublin to become the Dean of Saint Patrick's Cathedral but they continued a very loving correspondence. Then Esther inherited the house that is now Celbridge Abbey and moved there to be near him. He seems to have had mixed feelings about this....

'I ever feared the tattle of this nasty town, and told you so, and that is the reason I said to you long ago that I would see you seldom while you were in Ireland'.

Despite his fear of gossip, Swift came out to Celbridge quite frequently and the two of them would stroll along the river and then disappear into a 'lover's bower' that Esther had constructed on the bank. The original bower was destroyed when the bridge was built soon after Esther's death but it's commemorated by a summer house with a stone seat that was built later. Unfortunately the romantic story of Swift and Vanessa does not have a happy ending. He became increasingly involved with 'Stella', actually Esther Johnson, who he had taught when she was a child. The early eighteenth century was not a puritanical period in history but Swift was incredibly secretive about his love life and nobody knows what actually went on between him and these young women. Certainly Vanessa didn't know what he was up to with Stella and became so obsessed by it that she wrote a letter to her rival asking her what the story was. Stella then showed the letter to Swift. He lost his temper, jumped on a horse and rode straight to Celbridge where he slapped the letter down on a table in front of Vanessa and stormed out without saying a word. Vanessa died three weeks later at the age of thirty-four, some sources give the cause of death as tuberculosis, others as a broken heart.

At the end of the main street are the gates of Castletown House which, along with Russborough and a few others, is said to be the finest Palladian mansion in Ireland. It's certainly the largest – it has nearly three hundred windows. The word 'finest' doesn't necessarily mean the most beautiful. It means that in architectural terms it conforms most accurately to the strict rules of classical Palladian design. It was built in 1722 and the architect was the Italian Allessandro Galilei. It's the only house he built in Ireland. The client was William 'Speaker' Conolly, the Speaker of the House of Commons. One of the interesting things about

Evening paddlers,
Leixlip canoe club

Heron

the interior is that it has the only surviving 'Print Room' in Ireland. Print Rooms originated in England where they were fashionable among upper class ladies of leisure. The ladies pasted engravings and mezzo-tints onto the walls of the room and surrounded them with decorative borders. The one in Castletown dates from the mid 1760s and was the work of Lady Louisa who, when she was only fifteen, had married Tom 'Squire' Conolly.

The house was lived in by various branches of the family until 1965 when Lord Paddy Conolly-Carew put it up for auction. It was bought by developers who built housing estates in the grounds. The mansion began to decay until it was bought by Desmond Guinness in 1967. He started restoration work and made it the headquarters of the Irish Georgian Society. It's open to the public and contains much of the original interior detail and furnishings with the addition of collections of Georgiana from other properties.

The Liffey flows past the grounds of Castletown, past Barnhall Rugby Club, under a second Bridge, past a large canoe club and into Leixlip Reservoir. This is the final part of the 'Liffey Scheme' that we first encountered at Blessington Lakes in Co. Wicklow. And now the river is about to leave Co. Kildare and enter Dublin – for part of its course around here it actually forms the county boundary.

In Leixlip the river is joined by a major tributary, the Rye Water, which flows in from Maynooth. The Royal Canal crosses the Rye near the confluence on another rather fine aqueduct. On the embankments are a curious series of stone bordered ponds and the remains of an ancient swimming pool – the stones are coated with brown ochre. The water entering the highest pool comes from a thermal

Autumnal hues,
Leixlip Dam

spring and is not only warm but also mineral rich. This is the remains of one of the spas that made Leixlip and Lucan fashionable and prosperous villages in the eighteenth century. The only other memorial to this era is the name of the Spa Hotel, which still operates.

The area around this spa is botanically rich with fen plants and plants of lime-rich grassland, many of which have become quite rare. There's a variety of wild orchid species, dyer's madder, wild marjoram and vetch species. The plants support an insect population that includes the common blue butterfly, which is nothing like as common as it used to be.

The name Leixlip is Old Norse for Salmon Leap. The Vikings established a base in Dublin, and at the mouth of many of the country's other large rivers. They first arrived at the mouth of the Liffey on a raid in 837 AD but established a settlement in 841. They then pushed inland to trade and raid. They used small, light boats and had techniques involving rollers to get them up rapids and shallow places. It must have been quite slow going but if they got into trouble they could shoot back downstream to their base relatively quickly. They arrived in Leixlip over a thousand years before the dam was built and discovered that near the junction of the Liffey and the Rye Water there

was a cascade with a narrow neck that obstructed the migration of salmon. This was very significant.

History has rather neglected the importance of fish in the development of western civilisation. The extraordinary outpouring of Vikings from Scandinavia in the eighth and ninth centuries was almost certainly based on fish. They were skilled boat builders and users, they lived in a part of Europe that, at the time, teemed with cod, herring and salmon and they knew how to dry, salt and smoke fish so that it would last virtually indefinitely. This gave them surplus wealth, nutritious food supplies for long voyages and a valuable trading commodity – so they spread out all over Europe, deep into Russia, and as far as North Africa and even North America. Dried salt fish remained among the most important of trade goods in Europe for the next thousand years.

The amount of salmon spawning in the Liffey catchment over a thousand years ago was quite unimaginable. So when Viking explorers reached Leixlip and found the obstruction in the river where fish were concentrated while they waited for the right water conditions to jump up the cascade and continue their migration to the spawning grounds upstream it was like finding a gold mine. Fish penned up here waiting for a flood were relatively easy to net, trap or spear.

*Winter sunshine,
Lucan Village*

Our perception of Vikings in this country is extremely biased and we tend to think of them as merciless pirates with the devil's horns on their helmets. This is because most of the history we have access to was written by whingeing monks who were terrified of Vikings. In fact, up until recently, most of this history was also taught by the priests, nuns and brothers who were the spiritual descendents of the whingeing monks. As a result we fail to appreciate how much we owe in Ireland, a country largely uninfluenced by the Roman Empire, to these sea-going traders with a cosmopolitan culture. They built our first cities, introduced us to the concept of money and generally civilised us.

A little downstream of Leixlip the Liffey flows through Lucan, arriving over a long weir set at an acute angle across the river. It used to channel water to Lucan Iron Works. There is a fish pass in the weir. Small numbers of salmon still run the Liffey and the ESB operates fish lifts and passes in its dams. But the river is currently closed to all forms of salmon fishing in an attempt to let stocks regenerate. There is a rather fine bridge below the weir with a single span of thirty-four metres and an ornate cast iron balustrade. Nobody seems to know either its exact date or its designer but there is a clue in the fact that the balustrade was made by the Phoenix Iron Works of Dublin in 1814.

A small tributary called the Griffeen River joins the Liffey from the south in Lucan. At the junction the Griffeen is spanned by a small but rather complex bridge with the inscription 'built by Agm Vesey for ye public in ye yer 1773'. The 'Agm' is a shortening of a rather unusual Christian name that was used in the Vesey family over many generations. The bridge builder was in fact the Right Honourable Agmondisham Vesey. The same man decided in 1771 to demolish Lucan Castle, which he was living in at the time, and replace it with Lucan House. It was a thirteenth century castle, with many later additions, and described as 'battlemented and irregular'. His wife wasn't keen on the idea. She liked the old castle 'with its niches and thoussand other beauties' (spelling doesn't seem to have been the Veseys strongest subject). To placate her Agmondisham incorporated a round room in the grand new house for her personal use. At first this was a failure because when she was in her new room she felt 'like a parrot in a cage'. But eventually she came round and their descendents lived in the house until 1921. Today it's the property of the Italian government and the Italian ambassador's residence.

Around about here the Liffey abandons its meandering habit and sets off for Dublin in a fairly straight line through a shallow gorge. Considering the explosive growth of the west Dublin suburbs, the river banks are remarkably rural. A group called the Liffey Valley Park Alliance is lobbying to maintain this rural feel and open up the area for public access and recreation. They cite the precedent of the Lagan Valley Regional Park outside Belfast. It seems like an admirable idea.

The road through the gorge on the north bank of the river passes through an area called The Strawberry Beds, where there are several pubs and pub-restaurants. The name does in fact come from strawberry growing – the fruit thrived on the well-drained south-facing slopes of the valley between Lucan and Knockmaroon, though not any more. In the nineteenth century an expedition from Dublin to this area on a Sunday seems to have been very popular, particularly among what were described as 'the artisan class'. In season strawberries were served at tables outside the cottages on cabbage leaves in place of plates and with a portion of cream. This cost one old penny. The Dublin Penny Journal published a piece in 1833 that noted:

Survivors - Cottages at Strawberry Beds

... '*Of the various pleasant drives around the metropolis, that through the Phoenix Park, by the side of the Liffey, and the Strawberry Beds to Lucan, Leixlip and the Salmon Leap appears to be the most esteemed by the citizens.'*

There's a weir called 'The Wren's Nest' on this stretch of river. It's probably the most feared of all the obstacles on the Liffey Descent canoe race, and therefore a popular spot with spectators and television camera crews hoping for spectacular capsizes. After the weir the Liffey heads for Palmerstown, flowing under the lofty West Link toll bridge, and on to Knockmaroon and Chapelizod.

Chapelizod is the Chapel of Isolde, or Iseult. The medieval romance that tells the tragic love story of Tristan and Isolde is probably best known today from Wagner's operatic masterpiece, first performed in Munich in 1865. The story, in brief, is that Mark, King of Cornwall and a Norman knight, sends an emissary, another Norman knight called Sir Tristan, to Dublin with his request to marry Isolde. Isolde, a Gaelic princess, is the daughter of King Aengus. Partly because of a love potion administered by Isolde's maid, the princess and the ambassador fall passionately in love with each other. The wedding to King Mark does take place but the two lovers continue to meet in secret. Rather inevitably, they are found out, Tristan is mortally wounded and Isolde's heart breaks. They are reunited in death.

It's impossible to know how much of this story is fact and how much is fiction. But there is some evidence to show that the characters, at least, actually existed and have a real connection with this part of west Dublin. Most historians believe that King Aengus was a real person and that his Chapel-Royal stood where the old Church of Saint Mary now stands in Palmerstown. Part of the old sixth century chapel is also supposed to be incorporated into the fabric of Saint Laurence's, the present parish church. They also believe that he had a daughter called Isolde and some very early chronicles record the arrival of a Sir Tristan in Dublin.

And Chapelizod is not the only place name that recalls the unlucky princess. Close to here the mound on which the Magazine Fort stands in the Phoenix Park was originally called 'Isolde's Fort' and a nearby spring was also named after her. The Irish on the name plate for Exchange Street Upper, near Capel Street Bridge, is Sraid Iosoilde. The street used to lead to Isolde's Tower, a defensive fort which King Aengus built and named after his daughter. Apparently it was once a Dublin landmark because it became isolated on an outcrop of rock following an earth tremor. There is speculation that the fabric of the tower is still embedded in the buildings that have since grown up around it. In the Rotunda Room in the old City hall there is a fresco with a romantic depiction of Sir Tristan at the court

*Awaiting owners near
pub in Chapelizod*

Before the 'Off' at Trinity Rowing Club

of King Aengus – the scene is described as taking place on the forecourt of King Aengus' residence on Palmerstown Green.

If you stand on Chapelizod Bridge today you will notice that, both upstream and downstream, the Liffey still manages to insinuate a suggestion of the rich Leinster countryside into the urban sprawl. On the downstream side, behind the old pub, there's a mooring of small boats to remind us that, from source to mouth, this river is a vital leisure amenity. This becomes even more evident a little further downstream. Here the north bank of the river is bounded by The Phoenix Park and the south bank by The Memorial Park in which a number of club houses form one of the main headquarters for Irish competitive rowing. At the end of this stretch is the weir of Islandbridge and below this the river becomes tidal. There are only a few kilometres left to go, but there's a lot in those kilometres.

But before we start we must acknowledge the fact that here there is another dividing line. We have descended the upper reaches in Wicklow and the middle reaches in Kildare and we're about to arrive at something quite different. The Liffey becomes not just a tidal river but also a thoroughly urban one. No grouse, no kingfishers, but strata upon strata of rich history.

The story of Dublin goes back at least eighteen hundred years. In the second century AD Ptolemy of Alexandria marked it as 'Eblana' on his map of the known world, so there must have been some sort of significant settlement there at the time. According to The Annals of the Four Masters the name *Dubhlinn* dates back to 291 AD and then referred generally to the estuary of the Liffey, it seems later to have been used more specifically to describe a black pool at the junction of the Liffey and the River Poddle. The name *Ath Cliath*, referring to a ford, seems to be later – the first recorded reference to it is in 765 AD. But the tidal reaches of the Liffey were very different in ancient times, in fact it must have been quite a difficult site for a settlement that was eventually to become a capital city. The river was subject to torrential and sometimes devastating floods and these persisted, to an extent, right up until the ESB constructed the three dams in the 1940s. The old shoreline is commemorated in some old Dublin street names. On the north bank it ran from Great Strand Street, along Amiens Street and the North Strand; on the south bank along Fleet Street, through Trinity College, Fenian Street and Beggar's Bush. It then spread out into a sort of muddy delta, with several channels, before joining the Dodder and sprawling out to sea in the Ringsend area.

The story of Beggar's Bush gives an idea of what things were like just three hundred years ago. There was an actual bush here, a venerable hawthorn that appears to have survived into the early years of the twentieth century. It grew somewhere around what is now the junction of Lansdowne Road and Shelbourne Road. In the early eighteenth century the main port of Dublin and the principal connecting link between Britain and Ireland was the Pigeon House Harbour in Ringsend. There was only one road through the tidal marshes into Dublin – it went up the east bank of the Dodder, crossed it by a stone bridge in what is now Ballsbridge and proceeded on into the city. The old hawthorn on this road was hollow and beggars used to gather in its shelter to ambush their 'clients' on the busy road. As one account puts it ...

> *'So passengers from all parts of the world, alighting at Ringsend, had to proceed as best they could to Dublin, and here, by the Beggar's Bush, the beggars gathered, as*

they do in every port of the world, for their recognised prey, the foreign traveller.'

In ancient Dublin there were three fords across the Liffey. The first was Kilmohavoc, roughly where the weir is in Islandbridge today. It could usually be crossed on foot and is said to have been used by Brian Boru on his way to the Battle of Clontarf in 1014. Ath Cliath, the hurdle ford which gives Dublin its current Irish language name of *Baile Atha Cliath*, was just upstream of what is now Fr. Mathew Bridge. The third ford was near the mouth of the River Poddle which, before it was diverted into a sewer, joined the Liffey from the south on what is now Wellington Quay. It crossed the river on a ridge of rock known as Standfast Dick and, like the hurdle ford, could only be crossed on horseback at low tide. The first bridge seems to have been a wooden structure at the site of the hurdle ford constructed around the year 1000 AD – it was certainly there for the Battle of Clontarf because it's mentioned as the location of several skirmishes. In 1215 King John sanctioned the building of a stone bridge at this site. As part of the construction the mouth of the Poddle was dammed (which gives Dame Street its name) causing the famous black pool to fill with silt and disappear.

There are a surprising number of rivers and streams in the Dublin area, over fifty in fact, though all but the very largest are now largely in underground culverts. Only the Dodder in the south and the Tolka in the north have escaped this fate. Apart from the Poddle, which rises in Tallaght, the Camac and the Steyne come in from the south and the Bradogue from the north. The name Steyne, sometimes Stein, is interesting. It's Old Norse for a stone. Apparently the Vikings tied their ships up at two points in the city. One was the Dubh Linn where the Poddle joined the Liffey and the other at the pool where the Steyne joined the river, roughly where Hawkins Street is today. At this second mooring they erected a 'long stone', fourteen feet high, that apparently survived as a Dublin landmark for seven or eight hundred years – it's certainly marked on a 1655 map. The stone gave an old name to an area of Dublin and to the little river that once flowed through St. Stephen's Green, down Grafton Street and in front of Trinity College.

These rivers, pills and tidal marshes plus the fact that the Liffey was so prone to flooding posed quite a challenge. But gradually the engineers tamed the messy landscape, the Liffey was constrained by quay walls, the marshes drained and most of the little rivers paved over.

Mouth of the Dodder

As early as about 1650 Dublin Corporation refused to allow building on the river bank in order to allow for the construction of quays. By 1700 The Poddle, the Steyne and the Bradogue had been put underground, the markets had been moved to the north side and the north bank of the river was lined by quays from Arran Quay to Bachelor's Walk while the south bank had quays from Usher's Island to the old Custom House Quay and from Aston's Quay to

City Quay. This was partly to please the Duke of Ormond who wanted a broad highway running from the city centre to the Phoenix Park. But the end result was that the Liffey was neatly contained, more bridges were being built across it and the city centre began to assume the shape we know today. In 1713 Sir John Rogerson had a wall built on the south side of the river as far as Ringsend. But there was a gap between this wall and George's Quay which the Corporation filled in 1715, which is why it's called City Quay. The Pigeon House Road was completed in 1735 and the Poolbeg Lighthouse, with the wall leading to it, in 1792. By 1796 Grand Canal Docks were completed and the Dodder had been given a new course and its salt marshes reclaimed. The job was about done.

Now that we have an idea of how the Liffey was modelled and the centre of the city was formed we can continue our journey down stream, starting at The Phoenix Park. There's a bit of a mystery about the origin of the Park's name, which probably has nothing to do with the legendary bird that rose again from its own ashes. It's more likely to be an Anglicisation of the Irish language *'Fionn Uisce'*, meaning 'fair' or 'clear' water, a reference to springs that used to bubble out of the ground in the area. There is a letter in the correspondence of King Charles II of England dated December 1st 1662 ratifying the purchase of 441 acres adjoining the 'Phoenix Demesne at Chapelizod'. This land was to form part of the Royal Deer Park that eventually expanded to include Phoenix House and Demesne. The original house stood on Thomas's Hill where the Magazine Fort now stands. But the main land bank from which the park was formed consisted of the Kilmainham property of the Knights of Saint John of Jerusalem, an immensely wealthy medieval monastic order whose lands had reverted to the English crown when Henry VIII dissolved the monasteries. At one stage the park expanded to over 2000 acres on both sides of the Liffey, but it shrank back to its present size of 1752 acres (712 hectares) when the Royal Hospital was built in Kilmainham in 1684. Even at that, it's now one of the larger city parks in Europe, though not, as is sometimes claimed, the largest of all. Because its original purpose was as a royal hunting park it was stocked with pheasants and fallow deer, which are still there today, and surrounded by a sixteen kilometre long wall to keep the deer in. It's largely the work of the Duke of Ormond, who was Charles II's viceroy in Ireland. It was opened to the public by Lord Chesterfield in 1747 and extensively landscaped by a man called Decimus Burton between 1840 and 1850, when it was run by the Commissioners of Woods and Forests. Today it's run by the Office of Public Works.

The Phoenix Park holds an honourable place in the early history of motor racing and there are many sporting facilities in it today, including cricket pitches and a polo ground. It also contains Aras an Uachtarain, formerly the Viceregal Lodge and now the President's residence. The Deerfield Residence which was formerly where the Chief Secretary of Ireland lived is now the American Ambassador's residence. Other points of interest are the Zoological Gardens – Dublin Zoo was founded in 1830 which makes it one of the oldest in the world. The Wellington Memorial is a sixty-two metre high obelisk that has nothing to do with boots but commemorates the military exploits of the Duke of Wellington – its proper name is 'The Wellington Testimonial'. The Duke came from an Irish family and was born in Ireland, a fact he seemed to find rather embarrassing. He is once said to have remarked that being born in a stable didn't make one a horse. The Papal Cross was erected when Pope John Paul II came to Ireland in September 1979 and over a million people attended his open air Mass in the Park. The Phoenix Monument, a Corinthian column with a phoenix rising from the ashes at the top, was put up by Lord Chesterfield when he let in the great unwashed in 1747. Farmleigh, now the State Guest House, is on the edge of the Park. Ashtown Castle, a medieval tower house that was restored in the seventeenth century, has a visitor centre beside it which contains much more information. Finally the headquarters of An Garda Siochana are in the Park.

Just along from Phoenix park, at the busy bridges carrying traffic to and from Heuston Station, is Collins Barracks. It was the first building of its type to be erected in Britain or Ireland and because of this it was originally simply called 'The Barracks'. It was built out of granite between 1701 and 1760 as a result of a British government policy decision. Before this soldiers had been billeted on local households as lodgers. But then the political authorities decided that this was leading to dangerous 'fraternisation' with the native Irish and decided to start building barracks for them. Eventually it ended up as the 'Royal Barracks' with accommodation for three infantry regiments and one cavalry regiment, nearly five thousand men, plus some horses. In December 1922 it was taken by the Free State Army under General Richard Mulcahy and renamed in honour of Michael Collins, who had been shot at Beal na Blath the previous August. It was probably the longest continuously occupied military barracks in the world but today it has been de-militarised and is an exhibition space for the collections of the National Museum of Ireland.

Across the river is Heuston Station which was built in the 1840s as the terminus and headquarters of the Great

Southern and Western Railway Company. The reason, of course, that Dublin doesn't have a Grand Central Station but instead has several unconnected ones in various parts of the city is that they were built by competing private railway companies in the nineteenth century. The station was originally called Kingsbridge. Sean Heuston, who was shot at dawn on May 8th 1916 by the British authorities for his part in the Easter Rising, worked at the station as a minor employee of the Great Southern and Western Railway Company. The building was designed by Sir John MacNeill, who was engineer to the company. He came up with an early and rather fine example of a large Victorian iron and glass railway station in the form of a Renaissance palace. It has recently been extensively refurbished and had a Luas tram station added on to the eastern side.

Beside the station is Dr Steevens' Hospital, an even finer building and much older. It dates from the early eighteenth century. Dr Richard Steevens was Regius Professor of Physics in Trinity College. When he died, in 1710, he left his estate to his sister Grizel with the stipulation that on her death the remaining money would be used to found a general hospital in the city. But Grizel didn't wait. She kept just £150 a year for her own upkeep and used the rest to start on the hospital immediately. Johnathan Swift was one of the trustees and Esther Johnson, his 'Stella'

whom we met in Celbridge, donated £1000. It opened in 1733 and the architect was Thomas Burgh. He was rather a good architect who also designed the Long Library in Trinity College and Collins Barracks. The hospital is basically in the form of a courtyard surrounded by Italianate piazzas – the clock tower was added in 1736. It functioned as a hospital until 1987. It now houses Health Service Executive administrators. The change from philanthropic health care to administration may say something about the evolution of medicine in modern Ireland.

Downstream the landscape is dominated by the Saint James's Gate Brewery, the home of Guinness. Saint James's Gate gets its name from the fact that it was the Irish starting point for the pilgrimage to the shrine of Saint James in Santiago de Compostela in northern Spain. This was an enormously popular trip in the Middle Ages. There seem to have been breweries on the site since about 1600, if not earlier. But when Arthur Guinness moved in to town from Leixlip in 1759 and signed a nine thousand year lease at £45 a year on a small and not very successful one he put the place on the map. He only leased four acres but it grew and grew, swallowing up whole streets in the area. By 1838 it was the largest brewery in Ireland, by 1914 the largest in the world. It no longer holds that distinction but it is the largest stout brewery in the world. Annual production is

Movement in Time,
Heuston Station &
Dr Steevens Hospital

82.9 million hectolitres (50.7 million UK barrels) of several different brands. It is currently owned by Diageo PLC, a multinational drinks company. The history of Guinness and of the brewery is a massive subject. Luckily there is a permanent exhibition on the site called the Guinness Storehouse that tells the whole story in great detail and is one of Dublin's most popular tourist attractions. At the end of the tour you get a free pint in a seventh floor bar with a magnificent view of the Liffey.

Historically the brewery had a very intimate connection with the river, though the belief that it used the water outside the doors for making stout is not true. Beer is a heavy, bulky product and therefore ideally suited to transport by water. In 1769 Arthur got his first export order and six and a half barrels were sent to England by sailing boat from the Old Customs House below Essex Bridge. This was the start of a massive export business. 'Porter' got its name because of the popularity of the drink with the porters in London's Covent Garden and Billingsgate markets. By the second half of the twentieth century the company owned two full sized tankers, the Lady Patricia and the Miranda Guinness, dedicated to exporting stout in bulk from a jetty close to where the East Link toll bridge is today. Originally Guinness for export was loaded on to barges on a branch line of the Grand Canal that no longer exists

and taken along the Circular Line of the canal to Grand Canal Docks in Ringsend. Latterly it was taken straight down to the Liffey on its own light railway, using rather magnificent miniature steam locomotives. When the casks arrived at the river they were loaded on to steam powered barges for transfer to the docks, which could only be done when the tide was low enough to allow the barges, which had collapsible funnels, to get under the bridges. But the other route using the canal remained important for the distribution of the product within the country, using an extensive network of navigable inland waterways. In fact the last true commercial cargo carried on the Irish inland waterways was fifty tons of Guinness from James's Gate to Limerick in July 1960.

Of course Dublin is famous not only for the production of alcoholic drinks but also for their consumption. Dublin pubs are world famous and you can come across replicas of them all over the globe. But there are many fine examples of the genuine article on or close to the river.

Personally, if I were going on a pub crawl of half a dozen of the best of them, I'd start in Ryans of Parkgate Street. It's universally known to Dubliners as 'Bongo Ryans' – apparently this was the nickname of a previous owner. It's currently owned by a small restaurant chain so today there's a

Glass o' Porter!
Guinness Brewery

strong focus on food but it still serves a magnificent pint. There is, however, no truth in the rumour that they have a secret pipe-line under the river and into the brewery. But the outstanding thing about Bongo Ryans is its genuine and splendid Victorian interior, complete with snugs.

Now cross to the south bank and make your way to the Brazen Head in Bridge Street. This is one of several pubs claiming to be the oldest in Ireland. The statement that it was established in 1198 is a little dubious but there certainly has been a hostelry on the site since the Middle Ages and the current building is quite ancient. The 1798 Rebellion was planned, and betrayed, in the snug and Robert Emmet lived upstairs for a while. Today it is an attractive pub that serves food and has frequent music sessions. The cobbled courtyard makes it more smoker-friendly than most city centre pubs.

The Palace Bar in Fleet Street is a haven of civilisation located on the frontier between Temple Bar and the real world. It's a fairly small Victorian pub that can get crowded at times with well preserved exterior and interior detail. It's mostly known for the famous people who drank here but are now dead. Michael Collins frequented the front snug but most of the famous people were writers like Brendan Behan, Patrick Kavannagh and Flann O Br-

ien. And it has always been popular with journalists (who I suppose are also writers). In its hey-day R.M. (Bertie) Smyllie, the legendary editor of the Irish Times, would hold court here.

When I was a student in Trinity, forty years ago, I used to drink in Mulligans of Poolbeg Street. It hasn't changed much. They no longer bottle their own stout but still do an excellent pint of the draught stuff. Its Victorian interior lacks affectation and it's a little hard for tourists to find. So the atmosphere, which is created both by staff and regular customers, is normally polite and civilised. One summer's day in 1946 it was discovered by a small group of American tourists who came in and drank bottled lager. One of them was a young John Fitzgerald Kennedy who had just been discharged from the US Navy.

The Harbour Master, across the river and behind the Financial Services Centre, is totally different. First of all it's a new pub, established in the 1990s. Secondly its location means that it's patronised by strange creatures like hedge fund managers. It also focuses more on food than on drink. But the food is good and I'm including it because the main bar is located in a wonderful room, formerly the Dock Offices, that has been sensitively preserved.

Dockers were a thirsty breed and there used to be many pubs along the eastern quays catering for them. There's only one of them left, The Ferryman at 35 Sir John Rogerson's Quay. It looks incongruous among the new office blocks and survives by serving ciabattas and designer water to the people who work in the offices rather than pints of plain for sweaty stevedores. Yet somehow it still manages to retain the atmosphere of a family-run, working class Dublin pub.

But enough of pubs, it's time to return to the fountainhead at James's Gate and continue our journey down the quays. Just downstream of the main brewery the view up Watling Street is dominated by the 'Onion Tower', the tower of an old windmill. It was part of a wind-powered corn mill in the early eighteenth century. In 1757 it became part of Roe's Distillery, which was taken over by the Dublin Distilleries Company. Guinness's acquired it in the 1940s and restored the tower and replaced the weather vane, which depicts Saint Patrick. It's said to be the largest windmill tower in Ireland or Britain.

Across the river Number 15 Usher's Island is the main location in the James Joyce short story 'The Dead', which was filmed by John Huston in 1987. The house actually belonged to some of Joyce's relations – his great-aunts Mrs.

Lyons and Mrs. Callanan and Mrs. Callanan's daughter Mary-Ellen. When Joyce was growing up it was the location for the traditional family Christmas dinner where his father would carve the goose and make a speech and afterwards people would sing and perform other party pieces. The character of Michael Furey in the story is modelled on Michael 'Sonny' Bodkin. He was Nora Barnacle's consumptive lover in Galway, before she left for Dublin and eventually eloped with James. When Sonny heard she was leaving Galway he got out of his sick bed and stood under an apple tree in the rain to sing goodbye to her. This was probably unwise because he died shortly afterwards.

The green dome of the headquarters of the Incorporated Law Society in Blackhall Place started life as a school called The King's Hospital. The king was Charles II and he granted the school a royal charter in 1670. At the time the school premises were in Queen Street but they became very run down so in 1773 a new building was started nearby on the corner of Oxmantown Green but, because of the familiar story of 'cost over-runs', it took a very long time to finish. In fact the green dome specified by the architect wasn't finished until 1904. Up until 1923 the pupils of the school wore uniform blue jackets with brass buttons and yellow waistcoats and the school was commonly called 'The Blue Coat School'. In 1970 the school moved upstream to Palmerstown where it's on the south bank of the river beside the West Link toll bridge.

Just back from Arran Quay is the cobbled expanse of Smithfield Market. It's another part of the old Oxmantown Green that was declared a market place by an ordinance of the City Assembly in 1664. A traditional horse fair is still held here, on an informal basis, on the first Sunday of every month. The old fish market has recently been demolished but the fruit, vegetable and flower markets remain and are treasures of Victorian architecture. Smithfield is also the site of the old John Jameson Bow Street Distillery and the headquarters of Irish Distillers, which absorbed the Jameson brand and is now owned by the multinational Pernod-Ricard. There is a visitor centre where you can learn much about whiskey.

Whiskey has always been claimed as an Irish invention, though certain other countries may have been rather more successful in marketing it. The claim may well be true. The story is that about fifteen hundred years ago Irish missionary monks in the Middle East became interested in the way the locals made perfume. They mashed flowers and herbs and distilled an essence from them using an apparatus called an alembic. The monks fermented barley with yeast, basically a brewing technique that had been in use for many centuries already, and distilled the result in an enlarged alembic, which became a pot still. They called the distilled spirit 'water of life', 'uisce beatha' in Irish, from which whiskey gets its name. It became very popular all over the known world. Peter the Great, Czar of all the Russias, once remarked: *"of all the wines, the Irish spirit is the best"*, an early example of celebrity product endorsement.

Usher's Quay is on the south bank of the river. In 1737 a daily stage coach service to Athlone was started here, it was one of the first regular long distance public transport services in the country. It was a big success and expanded to serve towns and cities all over Ireland, including routes to Belfast and Cork. The huge coachyard at the terminus actually survived up until the 1970s. To cater for the passengers a hotel called Holmes' Hotel was built on the quay and it was said to be one of the largest hotels in Europe at the time. In 1843 the hotel building was bought by an odd sect called the White Quakers. It was a break-away group from the Society of Friends founded by a man called Joshua Jacob who thought the modest life-style of ordinary Quakers was far too lavish. He publicly broke all his mirrors, watches and clocks and sold all his property to make it easier to lead a simple life. The building was demolished in 1977.

Striking a deal.
Smithfield Horse
Fair

Bridge Street sweeps up a hill on the south bank. Near the top of it there used to be a lane called Keaser's Lane, though it did have another name. This information comes to us from William Shakespeare's favourite source book, Holinshed's Chronicle of 1577.

"This lane is steepe and slipperie, in which otherwhyles, they that make more haste than good speede clincke there bummes to the stones. And therefore the ruder sorte, whether it be through corruption of speeche, or for that they gyve it a nickname, commonly terme it, not so homely, as truly, kisse arse lane."

Crossing over to the north bank Church Street leads us to Saint Michan's Church, a popular tourist destination. It's a very old church, said to have been founded by a Viking Bishop called Saint Michan in 1095. The Vikings arrived in Ireland as pagans but, by the turn of the millennium, most of them were Christians. The current building is nothing like as old, dating from about 1685. The church has many interesting features, including a very old organ that Handel is said to have used when he was composing 'The Messiah'. But the main reason why tourists with a taste for the gruesome flock to Saint Michan's is to visit the vaults and look at the mummies. They're not really mummies but for some curious reason, never completely explained, conditions in these vaults preserve dead bodies in a dried and partially decomposed condition, in many cases with the skin intact. The vault consists of a tunnel plastered with lime mortar with a number of side galleries containing coffins out of which protrude body parts. The so-called 'Big Four' are in a gallery containing three 'mummies' in a row across the front. There's a woman on the right, a man with a hand and both feet cut off in the middle. Some people say that this was the punishment for a thief, others make the even more bizarre suggestion that the appendages were removed to make him fit better in the coffin. On the left are the remains of a nun. At the back of the gallery is the body of a man said to be a Crusader. The body is cut in half and he has one hand raised in the air. In the last gallery in the vault are the remains of the Sheare brothers who were executed for their part in the rising of 1798. During the Bicentennial Celebrations in 1998 it was decided to give them new coffins. Only then was it discovered that the British authorities had carried out the ancient punishment for treason and the brothers had been hung, drawn and quartered. For those with truly gruesome tastes, the conventional name for this ultimate execution method puts the three steps in the wrong order. The victim was first drawn – that is his belly was cut open so that his entrails spilled out. He was then hung, but not suddenly so that his neck was broken – slowly so that he asphyxiated. The body was then cut into quarters that, traditionally though not apparently in the case of the Sheere brothers, were interred far apart so that the victim would not be able to re-assemble himself on Judgement Day. I wonder who thought that one up.

To the east of Church Street are The Four Courts, an architectural masterpiece designed by James Gandon and built between 1796 and 1802. The four courts were originally the courts of Chancery, King's Bench, Exchequer and Common Pleas. The legal system was changed in the late nineteenth century, and again in 1924 by the Free State government, but the old name was retained. The building was damaged during the 1916 Rising and actually destroyed during the Civil War. In April 1922 it was occupied by Republican forces led by Rory O Connor. After a stand-off lasting several months the new Provisional Government made a concerted attack on the advice of Michael Collins. In the course of a week-long bombardment most of the building was destroyed. Then, as the occupying forces were surrendering, there was a huge explosion that destroyed the Irish Public Records Office in the west wing. This was a tragedy even greater than the destruction of one of Dublin's landmark buildings. It destroyed nearly a thousand years of unique and irreplaceable archive. The government forces claimed that the Republicans had done

it on purpose. The Republicans, who included Sean Lemass, said it was an accident resulting from the fact that they had stored all their ammunition in the archive office. The building was rebuilt and opened again in 1932 but they didn't make a great job of it, in particular much of the interior detail was not restored. This was partly due to a lack of funds and partly for the ironic reason that the original plans had been in the Public Records Office when it blew up ... or was blown up.

Wine was a remarkably popular drink in Ireland in historical times. Even as far back as the Middle Ages it was imported directly, mainly from western France, to ports all around the Irish coast. Winetavern Street, on the south bank, was the centre for the medieval wine trade in Dublin, though none of the wine taverns survive today. The quay here was also the site of what may well be the worst accident in Dublin's history. In 1597 a cargo of one hundred and forty four barrels of gunpowder stacked on the quay exploded killing a hundred and twenty people and causing massive damage to property.

Fishamble Street used to be called Fish Shambles Street but the cluster of sibilants proved hard to pronounce so the name was simplified. The word shambles has changed its meaning completely over the centuries. It used to mean a market and this was the site of the late medieval fish market. But medieval markets were a bit of a mess, which is how the word got its modern meaning. But the street is best known for a building that disappeared long ago, The Musick Hall. On the 13th of April 1742 Handel's 'Messiah', one of the most popular pieces of music in the world, was performed here for the first time.

On Lower Exchange Street, just behind Essex Quay, is another famous place of entertainment. Smock Alley Theatre was opened in 1662 by John Ogilby, Master of the Revels, as the first true public theatre in Ireland. It therefore played a major part in establishing our strong theatrical tradition and has international significance in the history of drama. It flourished for about a hundred and fifty years and David Garrick and Peg Woffington performed here in 1742. But in 1811 the church of Saints Michael and John was built on the site – recent archaeological and architectural work indicates that the theatre was not razed to the ground but that the original building was converted into a church. The church itself made its way into history because in 1829, after Catholic Emancipation, its bell was the first one to ring out the Angelus in Dublin since the Reformation. A Protestant Alderman of the City objected to this and went to the courts to have the bell silenced. He withdrew his case when the parish hired Daniel O Con-

nell as its barrister. But now history has come full circle – the church has closed and it is in the process of being converted back into the original theatre.

The actual river frontage along Wood Quay is dominated by the Civic Offices of Dublin City Council. This cluster of buildings, finally completed in 1994, caused considerable controversy. The original design envisaged four large concrete cube-shaped buildings that Dubliners called 'bunkers' and that were regarded as eyesores. The outcry was so great that the design was modified and only two of the bunkers were built. But a bigger controversy was caused by the fact that when the site was being prepared the well-preserved remains of the Viking city were revealed. Building the Civic Offices destroyed what was probably the most important Viking archaeological site in the world.

But the City Council must be praised for what it did recently on the opposite bank. The construction of the Liffey Boardwalk, a broad wooden walkway dotted with small and inexpensive cafes, attached to the quay walls and suspended over the river, would not have been a success even twenty years ago. In those days the Liffey stank at low tide, particularly in warm weather. But there have been improvements in the drains and sewers and today

*The Liffey
Boardwalk*

Sunlight Chambers

a mob of a couple of hundred people to attack the socialists in Number 64. They repeated the attack the following evening but this time the socialists were prepared and defended themselves with three revolvers and a collection of heavy objects which they hurled out of the windows at the mob. Eventually, whether accidentally or on purpose, the house was set on fire. When the police arrived the socialists demanded full police protection, which they got, and the mob dispersed. The press loved the whole thing and called it The Great Strand Street Siege. Irish politics were obviously more colourful in those days.

There is an extraordinary building on the corner of Essex Quay and Parliament Street called Sunlight Chambers. It was designed about a century ago by the Liverpool architect Edward Ould, who also designed Port Sunlight in Britain. Sunlight is a reference to a famous brand of soap made by the Lever Brothers company and this building was originally Lord Lever's Dublin headquarters. It's in a romantic Italian style with an over-hanging tiled roof and arcaded upper floors. But the really astonishing thing about it is the two multi-coloured terracotta friezes depicting the history of personal hygiene and the uses of soap. They have recently been restored. This building was very controversial when it was built, largely because the Dublin architectural community objected to the commission

the Boardwalk is a very pleasant amenity, a surprisingly tranquil place in the bustle of the city centre. It stretches from Ormond Quay to Batchelor's walk.

Behind Ormond Quay, Great Strand Street runs parallel to the river. In 1933 a group of socialists rented Number 64 as their headquarters. During Lent of that year Cardinal MacRory preached a sermon condemning left wing politics, thundering that: *"...there is no room for their blasphemies among the children of Saint Patrick...".* This inspired

Capel Street towards
Essex Quay and
Dublin Castle

going to an Englishman. So a magazine called *'The Irish Builder'* described it as *'the ugliest building in Dublin'* and, in a later article, as *'pretentious and mean'*. In fact it wasn't as incongruous in its day as you might think. There used to be a lot more of these highly decorated buildings in Dublin. I remember an even gaudier one, 'The Irish House', a pub on Wood Quay that was built in 1870 and sadly demolished in 1968. It had brightly coloured friezes showing, amongst other things, Grattan's Parliament, Daniel O Connell and Erin weeping over a string-less harp.

Parliament Street gets its name from the fact that it was the first street to be laid out by the Wide Streets Commissioners who were set up by the Irish Parliament in 1757. It was designed to be a broad thoroughfare connecting the river and Dublin Castle.

Dublin Castle isn't really a castle. It's more a fortified complex, a bit like the 'Green Zone' in Baghdad, and it was the seat of British rule in Ireland until 1922. Neil Jordan's film *'Michael Collins'* captures this aspect very accurately. Most of the architecture dates from the eighteenth century, although the site dates back to the days of King John who was the first British monarch to claim to be also King of Ireland in the early thirteenth century, and there are some modern buildings. One of its greatest claims

to fame is the mysterious theft of the Irish Crown Jewels from the premises in 1907.

It's been used for a number of purposes over the centuries. It was primarily a royal residence, the town apartments of the Viceroy and Vicereine. But it has also housed parliaments, military garrisons and law courts. When the Four Courts were being rebuilt after the Civil War their business moved here. Nowadays the Viceregal Apartments are called the State Apartments and are used, amongst other things, for the inauguration of new Presidents and sometimes the lying-in-state of dead ones. They are also a conference centre, particularly for important EU meetings, and when they're not in use they are open to the public and well worth a visit. Appropriately enough, the last people to have actually slept in the royal bedrooms seem to have been Margaret and Dennis Thatcher after a European Council meeting in 1979.

When Britain ruled in Ireland patriotic Irish people used the pejorative term 'Castle Catholic' to describe people they thought were being too friendly or supportive of the administration.

Today the complex is run by the Office of Public Works and they have some offices in a former stable yard. So

Equinox sunset,
Ha'penny Bridge

do the Garda Siochana and the Revenue Commissioners, who live in a twentieth century building at the end of Castle Yard. The crypt of the Chapel Royal is now used as an arts centre and concerts are sometimes held in the complex. The Chester Beatty Library, which contains one of the most important collections of oriental manuscripts in the world, is now housed in a purpose-built facility on the grounds.

The Ha'penny Bridge has had a lot of names since it was built in 1816 – Dubliners have always had a habit of ignoring the official names of landmarks and coming up with their own. It's been called Liffey Bridge, Wellington Bridge, The Iron Bridge and The Metal Bridge. Its current name comes from the toll of half a penny that was charged to cover the cost of building it and of buying a concession from the ferry-men who were once a distinctive part of Dublin life. Despite various attempts to abolish it, the toll was in operation until 1916.

Crossing the Bridge from the north to the south-side will bring you to the Temple Bar district, a maze of narrow streets laid out in the seventeenth century. A few decades ago, when the Liffey still stank at low tide, this was a rather run-down area of the city centre. But it has been developed as an artistic and cultural quarter and many of the cobbled streets have been pedestrianised. It also has a high density of pubs and restaurants and a robust and sometimes noisy night life.

O Connell Bridge was originally Carlisle Bridge. It was designed by James Gandon with keystone heads by Edward Smyth depicting the Liffey and Neptune, the river about to meet the sea. It was built in 1794 and widened and realigned in 1880, when the heads of Liffey and Neptune were incorporated into 30-32 Sir John Rogerson's Quay.. This was really the final stage in a centuries-long process that had seen the city centre moving gradually down river. Apparently if you stand in the centre of O Connell Bridge at the equinox the sun rises and sets precisely in the middle of the river.

East of O Connell Bridge it gets more difficult to write about the Liffey. This is because the pace of development is so rapid that anything you write is likely to be obsolete before it's published. But there are a few stable landmarks on the north bank.

Liberty Hall is a modest skyscraper of sixteen storeys. When it was built in 1964 it was hailed as a symbol of modern Ireland, though some Dubliners claimed that it leaned slightly to the right, an odd attribute in a building

Liberty Hall and
O'Connell Bridge

that housed the headquarters of the Trades' Union movement. The first Liberty Hall was established in 1912 on the same site in a building that had been the Northumberland Hotel. It was the headquarters of the Irish Transport and General Workers Union, established in 1909 – a key year in Irish labour history. The 1913 Dublin Lock Out was organised from here and on Easter Sunday 1916 the Proclamation of the Irish Republic was printed on the premises. The following day the main column of the Irish Volunteers and the Irish Citizen Army under the joint command of Padraic Pearse and James Connolly marched from here to take over the General Post Office in O Connell Street. They only left a single caretaker to look after the building but, despite this, the British shelled it the following Wednesday from the gun-boat 'Helga'. Today the keepers of the Celtic Tiger are considering demolishing the iconic 1960s building and replacing it with something more modern.

The Customs House is one building in the area that is likely to escape the developer's demolition men. It certainly should – it's probably the finest building in Dublin. It was built in the 1780s and is another design by James Gandon. Like the original O Connell Bridge, it has sculpted stone heads on the keystones of the ground floor arches done by Edward Smyth. There are thirteen river gods and the Atlantic Ocean. The Liffey god, naturally enough, has pride of place and is the only one that is female – so I suppose it's a goddess. Many of these gods, though not the Liffey goddess, appeared on the back of the original Sir John Lavery Irish bank notes. Gandon was an Englishman. At the time Dublin was regarded as a rather provincial city, at least in artistic circles, and the normal thing for the architect to do would be to commission a London sculptor to decorate his building. But he discovered Edward Smyth, a Meath man working in Dublin, who was a rather menial employee of his stone-cutting contractor. He immediately recognised Smyth's talent and skill and went on to employ him on all his Irish buildings. This made the sculptor's reputation and changed his entire life.

On the south bank, behind Sir John Rogerson's Quay, lies Windmill Lane. It gets its name from a windmill that survived there until the late nineteenth century. But its real claim to fame is as the site of U2's original recording studios. When they became famous, Windmill Lane Studios became a place of pilgrimage for fans from all over the world. The fans decorated many metres of wall outside the studios with extraordinary graffiti. There are still recording studios here, though under different management. There's also still a wall with some graffiti but true fans will tell you it's a fake and the originals have all been painted over. U2 are in the process of building an impressive new tower

Midnight reflections,
Customs House

close by, at the confluence of the Dodder and the Liffey, as their new headquarters and studios.

The modern development of the former docklands on both banks of the last few kilometres of the river really dates back to 1986 when the Custom House Docks Development Authority was formed by the government. The following year Charles Haughey introduced the Finance Act of 1987 which paved the way for the International Financial Services Centre to be built. The whole thing was expanded when the Dublin Docklands Development Authority was formed with a remit to regenerate a huge area of five hundred and twenty hectares between 1997 and 2012. This is a mammoth project with an investment of private and public capital estimated at seven billion euro. It will, amongst other things, create eleven thousand new homes, twenty percent of which will be social and affordable housing. This will grow the population of the area from seventeen and a half thousand people in 1997 to forty two and a half thousand in 2012. There will also be hotels, cafes and restaurants, a theatre and a marina, in fact some of these are already in place.

Many architects are involved, some of them employed directly by the DDDA and some from well known Irish and international firms. Personally I think the Financial Serv-

ices Centre itself is a fine modern building, as are some of the buildings and spaces behind it. There are other new buildings in the area that I would be less enthusiastic about. But one thing that seems to be universally popular is the development of the campshires on both banks. A campshire is the space between the road and the edge of the quay. In the old stevedore days they were covered in piles of freight and had rail tracks on them along which mobile cranes rumbled to load and unload the ships. This sort of dockland has been made virtually extinct by the invention of containers. Today the campshires are being developed as linear parks with cafes, outdoor sculptures and a dedicated cycle-way – a definite improvement.

Along this stretch two tributary rivers and two canals join the Liffey. Close together on the north bank are the mouths of the Tolka and the Royal Canal and, close together on the opposite bank, the Dodder and the Grand Canal.

At Grand Canal Docks a set of three old balance-beam locks allow vessels to transfer between the river and the canal. Today the area is a hive of development activity, as it must have been in the late eighteenth century. The original work on the canal didn't start in Dublin – apparently property prices were too high even in the 1750s. The first excavations were near Sallins, not far from the Leinster

*Old berthed at new
- Heritage boats at the
redeveloped campshires*

Grand Canal Lock

Aqueduct, and the Docks were only completed in 1796, a cause of much celebration with the vice-regal yacht being the first vessel to lock up from the Liffey and a ceremonial breakfast for one thousand guests served in a number of large tents. The canal took half a century to build and was an amazing engineering achievement and the first significant venture in the history of Irish capitalism. It started out as a state project – in the 1750s the Irish Parliament had a surplus of funds and, being reluctant to return this to Westminster, was looking for something expensive to spend it on. A canal linking the Liffey to the Shannon

seemed suitable. When the funds ran out private investors got together to form a company to finish the project. It was an early precursor of the great railway companies of the following century. But there wasn't much precedent for this kind of thing and the investors demanded unrealistically high dividends that bankrupted the company and the state had to mount a rescue package. This pattern continued even after the canal reached the Shannon in 1804. It was, of course, built entirely by hand (and by hoof – they used a lot of mules) and labour costs were the killer. Some of the work gangs had five thousand men in them. The story is that the Royal Canal, connecting the Liffey and the Shannon by a more northerly route, was started when an angry director of the Grand Canal Company stormed out of a board meeting shouting: "Damn you all, I'll build my own canal". This can't be proven but there is some historical evidence to suggest that it's true.

In the old days Dublin Port was notoriously dangerous. Sandbanks built up and ships continually ran aground on them. Efforts to solve this started in 1717. Restraining walls were built, extending out from both banks, the North Wall and the South Wall. The East Wall was built to contain the Tolka. The job was finally completed in the nineteenth century by building another wall starting on the northern shore of Dublin Bay in Clontarf and extend-

*Evening Solitude At
Clontarf - towards the
Pigeon House*

ing out until it nearly meets the end of the south wall. Much of the early nineteenth century work was designed and supervised by Captain Bligh, of 'Mutiny on the Bounty' fame. This system of breakwaters is regarded as one of the finest of its type in the world. It did solve the problem of the sandbanks. Much of the diverted sand began to deposit on the north shore of the bay instead and Bull Island and Dollymount Strand began to form.

So the last seven kilometres of the Liffey are walled in. It's the final act of human interference with a river that has dams and weirs across it, bridges over it, mill races abstracting from it and that provides the water for nearly a quarter of the taps in the country. Despite all these indignities it retains its character to the end. A clear stream hurries down the Wicklow mountains, empties into a great lake, pushes through the dam at Poulaphouca and takes a great curve through the countryside of Co. Kildare before it gets to Dublin. All along this looping course it has a strong relationship with the people who live near it, and has had since before history. It's a large river and a long river but, because of its strange course, if you stand at its mouth and pick your spot you can look south towards Kippure and see the mountain where it rises. At the end it flows proudly between the North Wall and the South Wall, past the towers of the Pigeon House power station, and out into the Irish Sea.

Somehow it's hard to resist the temptation to personify the Liffey. Many artists and writers have done this and James Joyce was so obsessed by the river that he had a map of its course woven into his sitting room carpet. Towards the end of *Finnegans Wake* his personification, Anna Livia Plurabelle, uses the amazing language that Joyce invented for the book to describe her feelings as, in her old age, she goes to meet her father, the sea.

'And it's old and old it's sad and old it's sad and weary I go back to you, my cold father, my cold mad father, my cold mad feary father till the near sight of the mere size of him, the moyles and moyles of it, moananoaning, makes me seasilt, saltsick and I rush, my only, into your arms.'

Dear Reader

This book is from our exciting new range of books which cover rivers in Ireland and includes:–

By the Banks of the Bann   **The River Liffey**

This new range is a development of our much complimented illustrated book series which includes:-

Belfast	Dublin's North Coast
By the Lough's North Shore	Blanchardstown, Castleknock and the Park
East Belfast	Dundrum, Stillorgan & Rathfarnham
South Belfast	Blackrock, Dun Laoghaire, Dalkey
Antrim, Town & Country	Bray and North Wicklow
North Antrim	Dublin 4
Across the Roe	Limerick's Glory
Inishowen	Galway on the Bay
Donegal Highlands	Connemara
Donegal, South of the Gap	The Book of Clare
Donegal Islands	Kildare
Islands of Connaught	Carlow
Sligo	Monaghan
Mayo	Kilkenny
North Kerry	Armagh
Fermanagh	Ring of Gullion
Omagh	Carlingford Lough
Cookstown	The Mournes
Dundalk & North Louth	Heart of Down
Drogheda & the Boyne Valley	Strangford's Shores
Fingal	Lecale

Cottage

Publications

Cottage Publications
is an imprint of
Laurel Cottage Ltd
15 Ballyhay Road
Donaghadee, Co. Down
N. Ireland, BT21 0NG

We can also supply prints, individually signed by the artist, of the paintings featured in many of the above titles as well as many other areas of Ireland.

For details on these superb publications and to view samples of the paintings they contain, you can visit our web site **www.cottage-publications.com** or alternatively you can contact us as follows:–
Telephone: +44 (028) 9188 8033
Fax: +44 (028) 9188 8063

For the more athletically minded our illustrated walking book series includes:–

Bernard Davey's Mourne	Tony McAuley's Glens
Bernard Davey's Mourne Part 2	Rathlin, An Island Odyssey